Drusilla Carr

BEYOND THE WIRE

Cover designed by Rob Williams at ilovemycover.com

I have tried to recreate events and locales from my conversations with Margaret Rose. This book is a biographical fiction based on actual events. Some names, characters, places and incidents are either products of the author's imagination or are used fictitiously.

Please follow me @drusillacarr5

First Printing: November 2020

ISBN-9798689943305

Dedicated to Margaret Ruth Rose (Cockayne) who shared her story with me and to the memory of her father Frederick Charles Cockayne.

Acknowledgements

With grateful thanks
Margaret Ruth Rose (Cockayne) has been most generous with her time and information. I count myself privileged to have heard, firsthand, her experiences in those long years in Dorsten and Biberach.

Duncan Swindells, author of the highly successful Scott Hunter Spy Series, is a writer who really understands the complicated business of editing. I am indebted to him for his expertise and generosity of time in this important aspect of my work.

Allan Skirrow shares my passion for History and has been most helpful in my search to discover the origins of the special quality which makes a Guern such a pleasure to know.

Georgia Boyd, a busy artist and musician, gave her valuable time to proofread and offer constructive criticism.

Prologue

She stopped talking. The room fell silent. Hands came together, slowly, hesitantly at first as if not quite daring to comment on what they had just heard. But then, as they stared at the tiny figure and realization dawned, the gentle ripple roared, stamping and clapping peaked and people, overcoming their reticence, demonstrated respect, admiration and empathy for the storyteller and her incredible tale. The speaker; Margaret Ruth Rose. The Tale; The illegal deportation of civilians from the Channel Islands to Nazi Germany in 1942.

✻✻✻

Part of a mixed audience that night I witnessed for myself the fascination with both the story and its teller. There were survivors of the war, elderly people who nodded quietly in agreement or sighed to themselves as they recalled a raid, a battle or a personal loss. There were the many, born at the end of the war and still wanting to know more about an event that had cast long shadows over the world just as they were making their entry. And then there were the young for whom, at the start of the evening, none of this had any real meaning beyond being the kind of story they might have read but not believed.

That night I could think of nothing else. True, there are countless tales of the camps and their horrors? However there are not many where the intention was not to exterminate and create an Aryan Race but punishment in the form of a wicked and unjust reprisal. They were not victims of the Holocaust but victims nevertheless and because theirs is the story of 2,300 and not the tragedy and horror of the 6 million it's a story that is not widely known. They were ordinary civilians caught up in a war that was not of their making. Lives were destroyed and nearest and dearest taken. It's the story of man's inhumanity to man. But it is also a tale of love, compassion, bravery and endurance.

✳✳✳

In this 21st century there are those who choose to deny the events of WW2, refuse to acknowledge the horror of the concentration camps and cannot believe that families were deported to satisfy the whim of an evil man.

For those people life is more comfortable without having to look at the past, but for the many still alive, who witnessed and experienced those war-torn years, all they ask is that their stories be believed and that it never be allowed to happen again.

✳✳✳

To begin to understand the events all those years ago we must try to put ourselves in their position, imagine how people with their background, culture, lifestyle and attitudes might have reacted. One question will always remain. How could it have happened? So, who were they? And to what extent does background, family, education, religion, lifestyle, sex and age enable us to cope better or worse when the very essence of life is challenged? Or is it purely about the ability to survive? And if that is so then attitude is more important than anything else closely followed by the need for shelter, water, fire and last of all food.

I was a child when they came. Men with marching feet and loud guttural voices. Men with steel helmets and guns. Chronologically I was almost a teenager when they left but with my emaciated, starved little body I still looked like a child. Emotionally I was a woman for in those few years I had experienced and endured more than most people in their entire lives.

That I would remember it for ever goes without saying. For some years it dominated my thinking, was the reason for decisions and attitudes and affected relationships. I have always understood why the soldiers from WW1 rarely spoke of their long years in the trenches. They had no meeting place. And nor did I. The truth is so far-removed from the lives of those around you that you wouldn't know where to begin. And so it was with me. I moved on, work, marriage, family with less frequent trips down memory lane.

And it was only when I was asked to give a talk on my experiences that I began to think again about those years, only this time differently. I was no longer a child, I was an adult and an elderly one too and now what I saw was with hindsight and coloured by time. I saw it anew, the memory of the pain and deprivation were still there but now as an adult I realized that what I had seen and not really understood as a child posed new questions.

The story as I had always known it was not enough, well not enough for me now.

I had no problem remembering when it happened. The date is engraved on my mind. 1942. But the how and the why left me with unanswered questions. The bare facts are there for anyone to read but we are talking about human beings, with minds of their own who were removed illegally from their country and imprisoned for years. What does it tell us about the people involved, captors and captees? And for me especially what did it say about my father, Frederick Charles Cockayne?

My biological father was somebody quite different. But as far as I'm concerned I am a Cockayne through and through. Adopted at birth all I know and have ever known is what I learned from the most loving of parents, Frederick and Ruth Cockayne. My adoption was never a secret perhaps because we lived on a tiny island where if you change your mind everybody seems to know. Perhaps it was because my parents feared I might be hurt if I suddenly learned the truth in later years. And as I grew to know about the moral code of Plymouth Brethren, my father's religion, it could have been considered dishonest, even a sin, to withhold the information. But whatever the reason we were always open about it. Never an issue for them nor me. And unless you show a special aptitude or talent linking you to your birth parents there is only one influence in your life, that of your adoptee parents.

So, as I looked to understand more about them and especially my father who played such an important part in my life right up to his death in the sixties, it is the Cockayne family who will supply some answers. And it is not enough to know names and places. I must look more closely at how they lived and what life was like long before the birth of my father or indeed his.

Cockayne is Anglo-Saxon and means idle dreamer. Dreamers maybe, but with their feet firmly anchored they had a habit of making those dreams come true.

The Year 1800, Yorkshire England

Blue. As far as the eye could see. Blue like the sky on a sharp winter's day. Blue like the sea. Not that he'd ever seen it but he'd once met a man who had.

He sighed, deep, contented and confident. The early morning friction of domestic life relegated to its proper place. The kitchen.

He always felt like this once the flax had flowered. He thought it was relief that everything was in its rightful place on time and that the cold spell at the beginning had not stopped the seeds germinating.

He would have been surprised to know that the colour blue slows metabolism and has a calming effect. Back then in the 1800's he wouldn't have understood any of that and the sheer hint of such an idea would have evoked some rich north country humour.

***

My father felt exactly the same when the tomatoes were covered in bright yellow flowers and the daffodils in bud. He would kick off his boots, wander into the kitchen, give a great sigh of satisfaction and kiss my mother. Plymouth Brethren don't go in for celebration but we recognised the signal that all was decidedly well in our vinery and there were smiles all round.

I doubt whether he would have understood any more than William that colours have special properties, although when the daffodils were in flower one felt his happiness and optimism. I can see him now coming in from the fields and filling my hands with flowers.

***

There was only one mantra for William Cockayne and so long as you came from Yorkshire you would have no problem understanding it or empathising with it.

"Ear all, see all, say nowt.

Eyt all, sup all, pay nowt

And if iver the does owt for nowt

Allus do it for thisen"

So, does that make him a mean, selfish man? Far from it. Careful, yes. And as far as William Cockayne was concerned there was nothing wrong with that. A hale and hearty Yorkshireman. Friendly, but bloody-minded, stubborn and argumentative he was in no doubt that he lived in God's Own Country.

***

The stubbornness I'd seen in my father and which would serve him well in the trials that were to come I had always thought to be a Guernsey trait and if there was one man who believed he was a Guern it was Dada. Was he perhaps something else as well?

***

Life at the end of the 18thCentury was scarcely a bed of roses. Every penny earned was the result of long hours of honest hard-labour and none harder than those spent working the land.

The son of a britches' maker, William soon found work on the nearest farm where he swiftly learned the business, soon becoming an expert flax dresser, something Robert Burns had aspired to be, the pay being commensurate with the skill.

In Spring and Summer on a small plot of land adjoining his weaver's cottage William grew and dressed his own flax and that of neighbouring farms. In the Autumn and Winter he used his top floor for making rope while his wife spun the thread on a treadle operated spinning wheel.

With natural daylight at a premium the family worked from dawn to dusk, only on the darkest days burning candles or making use of the more expensive lanterns.

His industry and expertise brought their own rewards. He squirrelled away his earnings in a locked metal box on the shelf under the piss-pot.

Just existing in the 1800's was a challenge. Conditions were harsh. The rhythm of life was dictated by the hours of darkness and the changing seasons. With no electricity, gas, running water or main drains even the simplest of human needs became a time-consuming activity. Going to the lavatory was scarcely problem free. The water-closet situated well away from the cottage served a whole row of dwellings and was no more than a plank of wood with several holes over an open bucket the contents of which when emptied were used as manure while the urine was sold to the local tannery. Everything had its price.

✳✳✳

A hundred years on and there were many cottages on Guernsey with water closets not very different. My home had a bathroom and flushing lavatory but I loved going to my cousin's cottage and walking up the slope to the outside privy with newspaper cut up and hung on a large nail. Primitive panelling covered the bucket arrangement and there were holes of different sizes to accommodate tiny bottoms. After my initial fear of falling through it was an experience I thoroughly enjoyed. What was a novelty for me in those pre-war days was something different and disgusting in the camp.

✱✱✱

Routine was essential. Every day had its prescribed pattern, with top priority the tending and dressing of the flax, spinning of the thread and twisting of the rope.

✱✱✱

Routine was essential too in Dorsten and Biberach for sanity and safety, and the only means of holding people together and controlling, to some extent, the constant bickering and fighting over the appalling conditions and shortage of food. Three times a day we stood in rows waiting for the roll-call and body count, our minds as dead as the cold in our bodies and when it was over all thought of animosity to each other had vanished with the cold leaving only a unified rage against our enemy and the indignity we were obliged to endure.

✱✱✱

Personal needs counted for nothing while bodily hygiene didn't feature on anybody's to-do list. A wipe down with a bit of rag by the outdoor pump was more than adequate.

The washing of clothes was a totally different matter. Linen, product of flax, was thought to be the natural repository of dirt and excess humours and so important was this that Monday was officially known as Wash Day. Water was heated in a set pot and poured into a tub with grated flakes from a bar of hard soap. Washboard with posser or washing dolly agitated the water, well-developed muscles scrubbed away while a two-roller mangle waited to squeeze out the water before hanging outside on a long line with huge dolly pegs or inside on a clothes horse that dangled from the ceiling. Certainly, until the arrival of the washing machine and for what appeared to be no particular reason, Monday remained Wash Day.

After Monday the week had its natural course. Ironing with the heavy flat irons heated on the kitchen range. The cooking, smoking, drying and salting of beef. The preparation of porridge and blue gruel with oats, cream skimmed off the top of the milk, and havercakes, flat oatcakes hung to dry on the kitchen clothes rack. And then there was cleaning and mending with the women doing all of this in addition to their expected contribution from the spinning wheel.

But the seventh day was sacrosanct and in a village where the pastor was not only head of his church but probably also headman in the community, there was almost universal attendance at morning service with the children following up with Sunday School in the afternoon where they learned not only the scriptures but some simple reading and writing. Playing games was not allowed and board-games were considered a sin.

✳✳✳

Another likeness. My father was deeply religious and it was this faith that sustained him during those heart-rending years in the camp. He was a member of the Plymouth Brethren, a movement which began in Ireland in the early 1800s and into which you are usually born although some people wanting to adopt their way of life ask to be admitted. It is unlikely that the early Cockaynes were followers so when and where did the connection start because my father was a preacher which suggests both knowledge and commitment?

✳✳✳

Christmas was not the celebration it became in Victorian times but it was important especially for people like William. Now was the time for looking forward to longer days and lighter nights, the opportunity to grow and dress more flax. It was a period of festivity, when sprigs of holly, mistletoe, evergreens and rosemary decorated walls and windows. But all the fun was saved for Twelfth Night when families met together to eat. If you were wealthy you would have beef or goose, if you were poor then it would be rabbit. But a rich plum cake with lots of sugar was an essential part of every celebration and women would husband their resources to have enough to make the special cake.

✱✱✱

For me Christmas was this strange time that other people celebrated and that we did not. The early Cockaynes may have enjoyed their Christmas cake but it was definitely not on the Cockayne agenda as I knew it. Make no mistake we were the happiest of families but Christmas and birthdays were not celebrated and whilst I was small I knew no different. But once I went to school and met other children I learned that our way of life was not the norm. Christmas just didn't feature in our minds. I see now one of the reasons my mother always walked me to and from school was more about her own anxiety than my safety in the lanes. She was concerned that I would make friends who would point out what I was missing at home.

✱✱✱

Education was expensive and provided by Dame Schools where a widow or middle-aged spinster taught reading and writing in a corner of the kitchen or underground in the cellar. With many it was not much more than a child-minding service with a bit of tuition thrown in by a woman with no more than basic reading and writing skills herself. Her charge of 3d or 4d for a lesson was a princely sum to a man earning 15shillings a year, the equivalent of £33 today.

William Cockayne knew exactly what he wanted and checking that the local Dame could actually read and write and conducted her lessons in a clean kitchen he enrolled his two sons. Although he had taught himself with the aid of the family Bible he had no time to teach his own children and was prepared to fork out some of his savings to have somebody else do the job.

***

My father was a self-made man. Educated very largely at night-school he worked all day and studied all night.

***

Of one thing William was certain. With flax ranking only second after food in importance there was money, real money to be made. He wasn't talking flax dressing or twisting rope and he and his sons were about to be a part of this.

Built on seven hills and watered by five rivers, Sheffield with its roots going back to Celtic Brigands and Roman warriors was something of a frontier region with a healthy respect for trade in many forms which was where William came in.

Unlike silks, satins and velvets, linen had no social barrier to climb. Everybody wore and used linen. The upper-classes used it for undergarments, the poor for both under and top garments. This was a time when people wore several layers of clothing and because knickers had not come into fashion, shifts, smocks and chemises were made of strong heavy material to stay in position and protect decency. Linen was long-lasting, washed well and became softer with the passing years. But in those days communication was limited and because flax was grown in small quantities linen tended to be produced and marketed locally. It was the niche William had been seeking, the perfect opportunity.

A new market-hall in 1786 was the place to start. William rented a space and armed with a couple of planks, a homemade trestle and some hastily constructed boxes he began what he saw as the real education of his sons into the world of business.

Both boys were used to being employed, able to knit large shawls to keep themselves warm and skilled in the business of picking flax and winding skeins of thread at the weasel or yarn winder, which measured each length with a popping sound.

Half a pound of tuppenny rice
Half a pound of treacle
That's the way the money goes
Pop goes the weasel
A penny for a spool of thread
A penny for a needle
That's the way the money goes
Pop goes the weasel

✳✳✳
I've never known the second verse but the first brings back memories.
I can see it now, guards, guns at the ready, in their watchtowers high

above the camp. My father peering at us from the other side of the wire and my mother and another lady turning the rope, made from the rough string from a Red Cross parcel and chanting Half a Pound of Tuppenny Rice for a tiny girl to skip. That was in the early days when we were still relatively strong. By the end of our captivity even that simple activity would have taken more energy than I had.

It was a ditty not lost on William especially the second verse. A penny for a spool of thread. A penny for a needle. As a buyer he winced at the price. As a seller he rubbed his hands with glee. It was much as he had always thought, the bread and butter money would come from selling things people couldn't do without. Needles and thread. For despite the exorbitant price of a penny there were always women queuing to examine the needles for strength and sharpness while promising themselves that this time they would take better care of their purchase and be less extravagant with the thread.

Soon he realized that he was barely touching the potential in the market-place. There was a real interest in looking at other things, like tape for the many garments needing drawstrings, or ribbons to decorate a Sunday bonnet, while buttons, despite every house having a button-box, were always in demand for new garments and for old clothes wanting a fresh appearance. It was a simple matter to add wool, pins and twisted rope for decorative girdles but bolts of cloth for home-dressmaking and furnishings fell into a different category and required more space. William would open a shop.

***

William and my father have so much in common. Both good business men seizing opportunities and making the most of them.

✳✳✳

Such a venture required money. Lots of it. And William was not short. Indeed one might say he was loaded. The trouble was it was stored in boxes all over the cottage, under the bed, below the chamber-pot, in the warming cupboard, on the kitchen range. Not only were these not safe places but he was running out of them.

Some stallholders used the new Mutual Savings, a handy arrangement but offering little in the way of good interest or opportunities to borrow. There was only one other option. The Bank.

Wearing his Sunday suit and flat cap and with his boxes piled onto a handcart William presented himself at the door of the town's only bank. An astonished staff watched him stagger through carrying boxes which he put on the nearest counter under the supercilious gaze of the head cashier.

When the last journey had been made, William removed his cap. 'Now my lad, tha'd best be about opening an account in my name.' The lad whose years numbered more like fifty than twenty flashed a warning look which told the office boy to fetch the manager who had been watching the whole proceedings from his window and was even now entering the room.

'Thank you, Smith, I'll deal with,' he was about to say 'this person' when something in William's gaze warned him not to go down that particular road, and he quickly added, 'this man.' He couldn't quite manage gentleman.

William waited, saying nothing but staring directly at the portly little bank official.

The manager hesitated. Normally in these circumstances he would have despatched the likes of William Cockayne quite speedily through the back door but there was something in the man's demeanour not to mention the pile of boxes which he had witnessed being carried in at some discomfort to the carrier. Was it just possible that these strange containers actually held money?

'How may I help you?'

'Tha can stop buggering about and tell yon lad to get a move on if tha wants all this.' He waved towards the boxes. 'Tha does deal in money? I want a bank account. And just so tha understands I've counted every penny.'

The manager moved to open one of the boxes and hid a gasp. He had no idea how much there was but if all the boxes were the same then this was not a bit of petty cash but quite a sizable amount. Could it be that this ordinary-looking little fellow with a load of misshapen boxes was about to deposit real money? 'I'm sure we can come to some arrangement,' began the manager only to be interrupted by William.

'Na. I'm after no arrangements. I can take care of those myself. I simply wants thee to look after this little lot until I'm ready to buy the shop. After that, well we'll see how tha does.'

It was at this point that the Manager of the town's only bank realized that he was the one under scrutiny and not the other way round. He signalled to the head-cashier and indicated the boxes.

William took a seat and watched the proceedings with interest and not a little concern.

And when it was done to the satisfaction of both parties and William had a bank-book it was the manager himself who escorted him off the premises with a warm handshake and the promise of best service at all time.

'Aye well, we'll see,' was the best William was prepared to manage. He had not been unaware of the change of attitude when the boxes' contents had been revealed and would keep an open mind on the merits or demerits of the bank where he'd chosen to leave his hard-earned cash.

✳✳✳

My father was a much gentler man in his dealings with people, and life in the 1930s was a far cry from that experienced by William Cockayne in the early nineteenth century. But there's a certain similarity between Fredrick and the admirable William and it's not just their tenacity but also their care for those nearest to them and for the way they provided opportunities for neighbours. Family always came first but after that they would help whomsoever they could.

✳✳✳

The acquisition of a market-stall was a big moment for William. He was now a member of that ancient guild of Haberdashers.

But the opening of a shop selling haberdashery and large enough to include material was an even bigger step providing a service crossing social boundaries and requiring its recognition in the form of a new and more prestigious appendage. William Cockayne and Sons were now Drapers.

17

The shelves were stacked with bolts of fine fabrics, silks and satins, wool and worsted, cotton and velveteen and with many shelves devoted to linen, that most versatile and commonly used fabric. And now one part of the business serviced the other as the buying of material was usually followed by the choosing of accessories to match, the right buttons, tape, ribbon.

The family took residence over the shop, no longer needing to eat and sleep all together in one room. Now when they dined even the children had chairs and William's wife divided her time between running the home and being on hand to serve ladies with unmentionables.

Business boomed. The single-fronted shop was swiftly converted to a double-fronted one when the next building fell vacant. When one of the son's wives showed flair for window dressing carriages queued with ladies all eager to see the colourful display of fine materials which would be delivered to their dressmakers or to inspect the hardwearing quality of linen for their servants to make into garments suitable for working in the dairy or serving tea in the parlour.

They had been respected in the weaver's cottage. Their expertise had been used by other flax-growers. Their rope was widely known for its quality and strength and now with the shop at the centre of trade in the middle of the town the Cockaynes were serving not only the poor but the rich too, guaranteeing a success that provided the *entrée* to a society different from anything they had previously known. As far as the aristocrats were concerned the Cockaynes were still trade. In the wider community they were people whose opinion was sought on a variety of civil matters and not just because of their

18

bank balance, although clearly that played a part, but because they were good businessmen and capable of making wise, informed decisions.

It was about now that they forged their links with the Athenaeum Club. Chess was a family game handed down through the generations with pieces lovingly carved from local wood and honed into polished surfaces by their constant handling over the years.

✻✻✻

As I read this I am reminded of my father, another Cockayne who continued the family chess tradition. He played it too in the camp in the long hours when our closest contact was through a wire, he in one part of the camp, my mother and I in another. And when it was all over and he returned to his island a broken man, broken in spirit, broken in health, he still played, gaining comfort from the concentration and quiet companionship.

✻✻✻

Chess players tend to be intellectuals and introverts. During long periods alone they become more self-aware and develop their powers of analysis. They see beneath the obvious and look at possibilities and variations. Useful in business and a lifeline of sorts in a prison camp.

So, William and his sons were people with their feet firmly fixed to the floor and although from time to time they talked of becoming a limited company and diversifying they were in no hurry to make the next move.

What brought about a change was the same thing which had moved them on from stall to shop. Space. The double-fronted shop with its spacious living quarters and storage rooms was no longer fit for purpose. The sons were already married and living with their wives above the business. Even if they moved out there would still not be enough room for the ever-increasing stock their fast-moving business required. While outside the street was regularly dangerously crowded with carriages waiting to deposit ladies anxious to be first to see the latest Cockayne offerings.

There was only one way to go. Up.

✻✻✻

The likeness again. The business acumen of these 19th century Cockaynes and that of my 20th century father who like the optimist he was saw opportunities where other people saw difficulties taking his modest beginnings to new heights. Unusually he was that rare combination of introvert and optimist, a quiet man who thought deeply but whose glass was always half full rather than half empty.

✻✻✻

Together with a few carefully selected investors a site was chosen for the building of the town's first emporium or departmental store.

And as they moved up in business so too did they move up the social scale. Upper class they would never be but with their money and their success there were lots of people only too glad to make their acquaintance. Now family walked the shop-floor greeting customers by name, keeping a watchful eye on staff and always on the look-out for innovative ways to improve the store's image.

It was an exciting, glamorous undertaking but as always the Cockaynes were not about to be impressed by their own success. They ran a tight ship so it was scarcely surprizing that almost overnight the store became an enterprise noted for quality, versatility and service. The Cockayne Emporium was a household name.

In the 19th and 20th centuries shopping at a prestigious departmental store was an event for which one prepared and dressed appropriately. Hats were *de rigueur* varying in creations from a *haute couture* milliner to the homemade version decorated with fruit or flowers.

Ladies remained seated while staff presented the store's wares for inspection and approval, after which purchases were parcelled and delivered by a well-turned-out youth with bicycle and basket or by a distinctive van with liveried driver.

The destiny of the Cockayne family was writ in stone. The eldest son would inherit, while shares and positions would be handed out amongst the rest. The family would continue to compound the business assets, their loyalty and commitment never in doubt.

That anyone should not want to be part of the Cockayne Empire was unthinkable. So when it happened the repercussions were profound.

Generations had moved on from the Dame Schools and for some time the sons had been educated at public schools where they learned not only to speak well but to see business in rather a different light and where they acquired knowledge of the arts and sciences, leaving some of them an eagerness for something other than walking the shop-floor.

Charles, the eldest, wanted to teach. An academic he had no interest in the family's history of flax-dressing, rope-making or the retail trade. One wonders if he really appreciated the fact that his lifestyle and superior education owed everything to the earlier

Cockaynes who had slaved for long hours in the fields and weaver's cottage. Probably not, the young have no time to spend looking back, their lives are all about the future. He longed for the quiet ways of academia, for hours spent poring over books and the rapport he would establish with his students.

***

So this was my grandfather, a man of books and learning not a man of the soil or trade. My father was both a man of the soil and a man of letters and proud to be in trade.

***

What Charles had not anticipated was the unbridled fury of his elderly father for whom the Cockayne Empire was everything, the zenith of years of hard-labour which had begun with a man's dream to give the best that he had to his sons. To Charles's father his son's rejection was the cruellest of blows both emotionally and practically.

A generous, some might say indulgent father in most respects but when it came to business he was a man of steel. His son should not turn his back on the store and still enjoy many of its financial and social benefits.

After a final plea, begging Charles to change his mind, his father disowned him, no halfway measures, no small allowance to keep him going. You either gave your all to the Cockayne business or you were out. And out meant exactly that. Out. No money. No family. No home and complete severance from anything to do with the Cockaynes.

Whether Charles had expected such isolation it's hard to tell. If he had any of the Cockayne stubbornness then he probably stuck two fingers up confident that like the bowmen of Agincourt he too would overcome. In the event it was not quite so easy. He had the education but not the opportunity and with no money or immediate job-prospects he did what many young men had done before. He joined the army.

***

My father did exactly the same although not for the same reasons. He was one of the first to volunteer in 1914.

***

A well-spoken, well-educated and privileged Charles was officer material. The military would provide the opportunity to become an instructor. Not the teacher of classics that he had envisaged nor with pupils whose parents could afford to pay for education in a prestigious public school but with young soldiers from all walks of life.

It was a wise decision. Charles loved the life. Used to the discipline of public school the harsh routine was no problem. He even liked the food thinking it considerably better than that he had enjoyed as a boy. Physically he had never been better and once he'd done basic training the army wasted no time in making use of his teaching talents. Military History was a natural for him and his rapid progress in the technology of warfare and military weapons secured him a place as an instructor.

He visited far-off places revelling in the different cultures, climates and customs. After a long tour abroad the regiment settled in Guernsey for a while. He had travelled so much, experienced the world at first hand so what was it about this tiny island that cast a spell that he was never to lose?

23

✳✳✳

It is said that if Shakespeare had ever visited Guernsey his sceptred isle would probably have been Sarnia. (Latin for Guernsey)

✳✳✳

Charles fell in love and not just with the island. She was a dark-haired beauty with all the warmth and charm that so typifies the local people. It was a whirlwind courtship and when the regiment moved so did Leah with Charles. In Ireland she gave birth to their first child, a son, Frederick Charles.

✳✳✳

My father. Not as I had always believed born in Guernsey but born to a Yorkshire man in Ireland. Was it at this point that the family joined The Plymouth Brethren with its Irish roots or were they already members? For my father whenever it happened it was an all-embracing religion affecting his every waking moment. And born in Ireland? One of several factors that could have saved him from deportation. So why, oh why didn't he take advantage of it? Was it really possible that he never recognised the truth of his birth and childlike assumed that like his brothers and sisters he was Guernsey born and that the deportation didn't apply to him? It was the only place he called home. His life, his work, his loves were about one place, dear Sarnia. It was a love that would cost him dearly.

✳✳✳

Life following the regiment was just about possible with one son but when Leah was expecting their second child the army that had seemed like the answer to all Charles's problems and had indeed given him huge satisfaction and opportunities was suddenly the obstacle to the life he now wanted with his wife and children. The regiment's posting to India sealed his fate. He would put in his papers and retire to civilian life. But what does a man do who has only ever know school and the army? And where does he go to do it? At first he looked for some teaching but what he had to offer was bound up with the army and of the few teaching posts available there were none suitable for him with such specialist qualifications. Now too with the regiment on the move the domestic quarters were no longer available. He needed a house and for that he needed more money than the little he had stashed away for a rainy day. When you were in the services and serving Queen and country rainy days seemed few and far between.

❊❊❊

My father loved us dearly but he would never have contemplated resigning his career in the army or any other career. He would have thought it his duty to continue serving or working, providing for his family in the best way he knew how. Experiencing at first-hand the struggle to make ends meet he had a deep respect and gratitude for the work that he did and even when he was truly prosperous he never lost that humility. And there was something else, there was a toughness that was lacking in Charles. Was it that life had been too easy with the wealth of the Cockaynes behind him and that when he defied his father he did so with the arrogance of youth and without the knowledge of what such a step would mean? In my father I see a steely determination born out of need, something that didn't come naturally to Charles who lived through his emotions with little heed to the practicalities of life.

It was Leah who came up with the answer. They would go back to Guernsey in time for the birth of their second child and Charles would find work there. The Guernsey Steam Railway was flourishing and had a vacancy. Charles embraced it and he and the family settled down to an idyllic life on the island enjoying the beautiful landscape and the nearness of Leah's family. Why they left Guernsey in 1900 just after the birth of Winifred their sixth child is unclear. Did Charles tire of life on an island? Did he lose his job? Did he at last long to be near his parents and back to roots? Was it just a strange coincidence that a job on the mainline railway should be back in Yorkshire?

Whatever the reason Charles moved his family into a small cottage not far from the railway station where he now worked. It was not a joyful home-coming, well certainly not for Leah, who missed her relations and now without their support had a large young family to look after by herself, not to mention leaving a climate where all the year round you might expect an average of five hours sunshine. Life in Yorkshire was a far cry with its damp cold winds and winter snows. Even the people were different, their hardened living conditions making them tough in a way Leah had never known.

What happened next was to change the family's life for ever.

The station platform was crowded. What exactly Charles was supposed to be doing at that moment, we don't know. What we do know is that a young girl either jumped, fell or was pushed onto the line in front of an oncoming train. Giving no thought for his own safety Charles leapt after her saving her life and sacrificing his own. It was the heroism of a moment and the destruction of Leah's happiness and that of their children.

✳✳✳

I know what it is like to be a young child and lose a parent. My heart aches as I think of my father, now the oldest child with brothers and sisters and a grieving mother all recently removed from their home in Guernsey and living in a county where even the speech was a rough incomprehensible dialect. Surely now their grandfather would come to their aid.

✳✳✳

We can only begin to imagine the horror of the situation. Losing a loved one in any circumstance is bad enough but to lose somebody in this particular way is something completely different. How did Leah manage to cope with her own grief and with the nightmare scenario of telling her family how their father had died? How did she justify the man's courage to young children only concerned with Daddy not being there anymore? It was impossible to spare them the details for it was the talk of the neighbourhood and headline in every newspaper.

✳✳✳

Strange that even years on my father never spoke of it. Too painful and locked away? Or conveniently forgotten?

✳✳✳

The Cockaynes must have been fully aware of the tragic death. Did they make contact, offer help? Did Leah seek their assistance not for herself but for her fatherless children? Did she ask and was refused? Was it that, still bitter at the family's treatment of her husband, she had no intention of ever asking them for anything? Did she indeed refuse any help they might have offered?

I can't help wondering whether the old man, when faced with the knowledge of his grandchildren could have turned them away. His own kith and kin. And as I learn more about my father I am struck by his likeness to those early Cockaynes who struggled and strived and made their fortunes on the land and in trade. At this point he seems much more like the Cockaynes of soil and shop than his own father.

***

There was only one thing for Leah to do. She must return to her island home, back to Guernsey, where she had family and friends and where despite having no real money she knew she would be able to bring up her children.

Quite how she managed to achieve this it's hard to tell. She was a widow and no longer entitled to live in Guernsey. Although a British Crown Dependency, the Bailiwick of Guernsey has its own legal system much of which dates back to Feudal Normandy with a rigid policy regarding the rights of residency deeming that the island's prosperity depended on a low tolerance of crime, vagrancy, debt and residency. Those on hard times and widows whose husbands had not been born on the island were not encouraged to stay.

***

What kind of fate is it that twice in my father's lifetime his residency on Guernsey has been in question?

***

Somehow Leah overcame this problem, possibly legally, possibly not, but back to the island she returned with her large family. Most of the children were under the age of nine with the youngest one still not

28

weaned and Leah grieving the loss of her husband who had been the gentlest of men, her lover and her friend.

It was a wise decision. She was after all a true Guern.

***

My biological parents were both born and bred in Guernsey, so that I too am a Guern and proud of it. Wherever I have travelled for work or pleasure I have never felt far from my roots. People who aren't from the Channel Isles say there is a special quality about the locals, something that embraces others. They speak of a warmth and compassion but of something else too, something they find hard to define, a corporate spirit that prevails.

***

An island measuring 25square miles, The Bailiwick of Guernsey covers Alderney, Sark, Herm and Jethou and is a British Crown Dependency, not as many people believe annexed by England but part of the Duchy of Normandy and therefore of considerable importance politically and strategically. Consequently, the Queen is known on the island as the Duke of Normandy. It is governed by a Bailiff who is responsible to the monarch for good government.

Roughly triangular in shape and situated 30miles west of Normandy, Guernsey consists entirely of primitive rock. Granite, hard to the north and gneiss to the south. With a temperate oceanic climate and at least 2,000 hours of sunny weather every year its environmentally rich inter-tidal zone and tidal variations make for fast currents and dangerous local waters.

But it's the history which is really challenging. What was it that attracted early man to this tiny island stuck out in the English

Channel? Without the interference of technology, were ley lines the repositories of an energy too powerful to be resisted? And is it this same force which accounts for the nature of the people? Neither French nor English and certainly not a strange mixture of both, there is a warmth, generosity and openness which is unlike either nation.

Wherever you look there are ancient sites, stone circles, standing stones, and dolmens. Many believe ley lines criss-cross the island in straight geometric alignments, commonly known as energy lines and which appear to have been deliberately used by early settlers.

So it was that despite the sadness surrounding their return and Leah's fears about their future there was a feeling of relief as the boat docked. They were home, back where they belonged, for all the children with the exception of Frederick had been born on the island and even he had spent so much of his short life on Guernsey that he wrongly assumed that he too was a Guern.

✷✷✷

It was a belief that was to have grave consequences and was the ultimate destruction of his life.

✷✷✷

All he knew was that he loved this tiny island. These 9 by 3 miles were the mecca of his existence. Guernsey, dear Sarnia, for him his home, his paradise.

Too young to analyse his feelings or to even want to he did not realise that he had been bitten by the "small island bug" the x factor that makes islands so important to some people. Was it size, smallness, the feeling of being in a prescribed area, a wonderful coastline, and a climate that owed nothing to other places? Or was it about the people who enjoy a feeling of security and well-being not shared by those on a larger landmass?

At first like any other small boy returning after an absence to a well-remembered place Frederick just revelled in being there. His mother, too tired emotionally and physically, was happy to let the older children wander off. So long as they understood the need to have respect for the sea they could not come to harm.

Only people who know Guernsey can begin to appreciate the magnificence or danger of those powerful waves, sometimes as high as eighteen feet crashing down on the beach. A spectacle breathtakingly beautiful to behold but with life threatening consequences to the unsuspecting holidaymaker or small child. The English Channel is one of the busiest sea-lanes in the world. It is also one of the most treacherous.

For a week or two Leah basked in the attention of her family and friends. There were invitations from everywhere. People conscious of the tragic circumstances which had brought the family back to Guernsey and anxious to help in whatever way they could. There were parcels of clothing for the boys, bits of extra furniture and food, lots of it. Bean Jar, a cheap and nourishing meal made with pork belly, haricot and butter beans, carrots and onions. Conger soup. Guernsey Gâche, a delicious fruit bread and Gâche Melée a scrumptious apple pudding. And then there were ormers, mussels and lobster from the sea and plenty of promises to take Frederick to find these for himself.

Guernsey Gâche. My mouth begins to water. I thought of it often in the camp when we were starving and today it's one of the first things I fancy as soon as I'm back on the island.

***

Soon though this euphoric period had to end. The kindly islander had his own concerns and the older children must go to school. Leah, with the two youngest still at home must try to find some work to enhance the meagre pension provided by the railway company. With no real skills and no time to implement them she could only do domestic work and even that was almost impossible with no one to care for the children. In a largely peasant community few people could afford to pay someone else to do the work they should rightly do themselves. Eventually she found a little mending and ironing but it was too spasmodic to be of much help and so it was to her eldest son, Frederick that she turned.

***

I see now the reason for my father's commitment to his business, his heightened sense of responsibility and why he coped as he did in the camp. Life had been his teacher and a hard taskmaster at that.

***

The truth dawned gradually upon the boy. He heard his mother weeping in her room when the children were in bed. Thinking it was for the loss of his father he would go to her and hold her awkwardly in his arms begging her not to cry. But soon he realised that his father was only part of her misery, the plight of her children uppermost in her mind. And one evening she told Frederick the extent of their problem.

It was a heavy burden for a boy still at school. Not only was he Leah's emotional prop as he tried to stop her weeping but her financial poverty demanded practical solutions that he was ill-equipped to provide. Whilst he pondered he dug over the garden, finding energy in the physical effort and taking a kind of comfort from the planting of seeds he had scrounged from friends and neighbours. At least they could start providing some of their own food. But what about paying the rent and repairing shoes?

He had to find some work but who would employ a boy still not in his teens?

Surprisingly quite a few people. Nothing regular of course. All odd jobs from mucking out the pigsty to chopping wood and cleaning the chicken pen. Pennies in return but something to put in the pot that stood over the kitchen range. They were high days and holidays when either Leah or Frederick earned a little extra. Sometimes enough to buy the ingredients for Leah to make a Guernsey Gâche.

✱✱✱

So this was why my Father always found work for a boy looking for odd jobs. He'd been there himself. I know too now why he made such a fuss when my mother baked a Guernsey Gâche. Shades of his past.

✱✱✱

But Frederick was fast approaching the age when he might leave school. He couldn't wait. Not because he didn't like learning, far from it. Above all things he wanted to improve himself, wanted to earn a worthwhile living and provide for his widowed mother. But education would have to wait while he found something to swell the domestic coffers.

But what to do? With no father to guide him he started to explore just what the island had to offer. As soon as school was out and unless he had a job to go to, he wandered the island, trying to discover what opportunities there were for a boy like himself.

On an island built on a rock, stone must surely play a big part both locally and perhaps as an export. Frederick loved the colourful local houses in the blue-grey Bordeaux Diorite and the red-brown Cobo Granite. He promised himself that one day he would build his own house and not have to worry about rent ever again.

***

And he did build his own house but I had no idea just how important it was to him. So much of our childhood influences our actions long after the initial moment has passed. No wonder my father regarded his promise to build my mother a house a binding commitment.

***

Frederick began to notice how much stone there was and not just the houses. As he wandered around the island he saw the large numbers of Dolmens or tombs. In St.Martin's he found La Gran'mère du Chimquière, a standing stone looking strangely like a woman with breasts, curls and beads and dating back to the Neolithic Period with Roman additions. Official buildings, walls and walkways were often stone and of such quality that much had been exported to London where some of its finest buildings and roads were Guernsey stone. What finally convinced him was a strange story of a journeyman stonecutter who worked on the island for some years before returning to London where he spotted Guernsey granite being badly laid and suggested how the process could be improved. The contractor heard him and offered him work. In no time he became a wealthy contractor himself, an Alderman of the City and finally Lord Mayor. Frederick's imagination was fired. If a stonecutter could do it, so could he.

His enthusiasm lasted only a few days when he noticed how weary the men were by the end of a shift, the way the chalk covered their clothes, the accidents in the quarries and heard the raucous coughs that racked their bodies. What had seemed like the perfect solution to his mother's problems was not to be countenanced. Hadn't there been enough tragedy in the family without his working in an accident-prone environment or where he might contract a cough which would potentially shorten his life?

I can imagine my Father coming to this sensible solution but the idea that he should even contemplate working in a quarry has given me some amusement. I can't think of anyone I know less suited to that occupation.

✳✳✳

Having discounted working at one of the many quarries Frederick's thoughts turned to the services. He still had vague recollections of his father in uniform and like any boy his age the glamour of the army attracted, as did the opportunity to travel and while the pay wouldn't be great at least it would be regular. And he would work hard to get promotion. And was there a secret longing to be just like his dad?

✳✳✳

He was always interested in the army and when, in 1914, war was declared he couldn't wait to join up.

✳✳✳

So what stopped him? The same thing which had stopped his working in a quarry. An incredible sense of responsibility, amazing in one so young. He was the male head of the family and in those days the role of women and society's attitude to them was different. Frederick knew his place was at home. He recognised his mother's needs as being far beyond the earning of money. She wanted his physical presence and often when the younger children were in bed the two of them would sit together discussing the day and planning what to do in the future.

His favourite places were down by the sea, in one of Guernsey's many coves, watching the waves roaring over the stones and listening to the fishermen telling tales as they mended their nets. He learned how to gut fish and if he was lucky he might go home with one big enough to cook for tea. He watched the painting of the boats when it was too rough to sail. And childlike he saw something he really wanted. He wanted a sweater, the kind the fishermen wore.

✳✳✳

I never had one. By the time I came along my father had enough money to buy me beautiful handmade clothes and a sweater of the kind worn by local workmen was not on the list. My father would wear one but only when busy in the vinery. Interesting when you think what expensive fashion items they have become.

✳✳✳

It is said that Guernsey knitwear was much sought after even in royal circles, Elizabeth 1st and Mary Queen of Scots both had stockings made from this particular oil-treated yarn. When Nelson saw the sweaters worn by the Guernsey sailors in his navy he gave orders that they become standard issue.

But it was when Frederick looked more closely at the sweaters and questioned the unusual stitches in the knitting that he learned a rather different story. The sweaters, handknitted in the round with eight needles creating a tube had individual patterns representing the sea and the ships that sailed her. The ribbing at the top mirrored a sailing ship's rope ladder, a garter stitch panel showed the waves and the stitches on the shoulder were pebbles, stones and sand. But round the waist there was something else, a design that identified a particular area of the island. Its purpose, to help identify the dead as they were washed ashore after shipwreck. Picturing his mother identifying him, he discounted it immediately.

When the answer to his quest for employment came, he didn't recognise it as such. It was a small job after school and on Saturday mornings. A means to earn a bit of extra pocket money. Well, other boys might call it pocket money. His went straight into the big pot on the stove. Sometimes his mother would slip him a small coin, probably a farthing.

✳✳✳

I remember farthings, the monarch's head on one side and a robin on the other. There were four farthings in the old penny and today the farthing would be worth a tenth of a new penny.

✳✳✳

Occasionally, very occasionally, Frederick would treat himself to a large sweet like a Gobstopper that would last a long time but more often would buy something to share with the other children. A cone-shaped bag handmade by the shopkeeper and full of tiny sweets like Dolly Mixture.

The job was at one of the local vineries, greenhouses which had housed grapes in the past but were now being used for the growing of tomatoes, becoming more and more popular in the United Kingdom markets. It was nothing special sweeping up and wiping down trays and worktops. At first he did just what was expected, his interest limited to giving satisfaction so that he would be asked back whenever they needed a boy for odd jobs. But then one day, waiting for the grower to finish, Frederick watched the process and saw how the man enjoyed working the soil in his hands. 'Can I feel?' he enquired.

The man laughed and indicated for Frederick to try his hand.

Frederick felt it trickle through his fingers. He spent plenty of time in his own garden digging out heavy earth and removing stones but this was different, the soil was soft and smooth, almost caressing his skin. 'Do you mind if I watch?'

'Do what you like. It's your time now not mine.'

After a bit the man passed him a pot. 'Copy me.'

Frederick followed as the man working a tray with 250 studs cut out into a bed of soil dropped a seed into each, before covering and watering. There was something so gentle about it all, the process, the neat, clean surroundings and the quiet voices of those who worked there as if they feared too much noise might upset the plants. To the young boy coming from a house full of boisterous children with a stressed mother struggling to maintain some sort of order and beset and bothered by ever increasing financial burdens, it was like being on holiday. For a few minutes he knew what it was to relax.

That night he spoke to his mother. She listened patiently trying to share his enthusiasm. Although she was too kind to tell him, she didn't really care what he did provided it was honest labour. They needed the money, it was as simple as that. And with a bit of luck it wouldn't be too many years before Jack was making his contribution as well. 'See if he'll take you on.'

The next day Frederick was there as soon as school finished. 'I don't need anyone full time.' The man turned away. 'Sorry lad,' flung over his shoulder.

'An apprentice?' queried Frederick. It was something he'd heard one of his uncles mention quite recently. You learned a trade, got paid a little and were guaranteed a job at the end of several years.

The man turned back. 'An apprentice?'

'Yes. You take me on and pay me what you can afford. Well, enough to satisfy my mother. And you teach me the business.'

An apprentice. Now that was something different. The boy would be tied to the vinery for an agreed number of years during which time he could do what he did now only more of it with the odd lesson thrown in. It looked like a win win for the man. But to make it seem as if he was doing a favour he took his time thinking about it.

A bargain was eventually struck and as the doors closed on his education Frederick began his life in the nearby vinery.

✳✳✳

Poor father. I see now what motivated his thinking, and why he wanted so much for those he loved. Why he set so much store on being able to provide not just enough but the best. He had known what it was like to go without and he had been old enough to understand the pain and anguish of his poor mother. But I don't think I ever heard him complain about those early days and looking back I realise how non-judgemental he was. Even in the worst times that were to come he refused to act as judge and jury.

***

In actual fact it was an arrangement that suited both parties. The boss had a skivvy to do all the unskilled jobs of a greenhouse and they were many, often heavy and wet. In return Frederick began to learn how to grow tomatoes. The lessons were haphazard but satisfying due to their practical nature. He learned the delicate business of pricking out and transplanting. He learned how to pick, grade and pack using wicker baskets with pink tissue for the smooth and perfect tomatoes and white for the rough. The soil which he had so enjoyed that first day had its own problems and every year they would hire a boiler a bit like a traction engine to steam clean and sterilise before the fresh batch of seeds could be planted. There was much more to tomato growing than he had ever expected but as he learned new skills he was allowed to take part properly, earning praise from his boss who quickly realised what a wise decision it had been to take on young Cockayne as an apprentice.

Soon though the young Frederick realised that this practical education was not going to be enough. With his academic education having been short-lived Frederick knew he needed to go back to school. With what little money he squirrelled away at the end of the week, he raised enough to go to night-school where he took up his studies again concentrating at first on English, haunting the library in the evening and reading long into the night. He had always liked

Maths and now at night-school he learned Geometry and Algebra and borrowed books on quick methods to solve problems.

When he finished the course he was bitten by the bug to learn more. He was determined that one day he too would own a vinery and saw a future with not one but several, and possibilities to diversify. All of this he kept to himself but in anticipation of that time he signed up for lessons in book-keeping, land management, horticulture and floriculture. The history of the tomato never ceased to fascinate, especially how the Spanish, after their conquest of the Aztec Empire introduced the plant to Europe where it was much admired but never eaten as it was believed to be poisonous and only suitable for decoration.

✳✳✳

A chip off the old block, as akin to the early Cockaynes as his father had been alien. My father would have been everything his grandfather could have wanted. Committed to learning a business. Single-minded in the pursuit of success. And as for turning his back on the family emporium. I don't believe it would ever have happened. How sad that they were never to meet.

✳✳✳

The family were Methodists, regular at chapel and taking part in all activities. At a time when not many people could boast a decent education young Frederick soon came to the notice of the elders. The boy might be young but he spoke well and knowledgeably. He was invited to read the lesson and collect the offertory. And other people were noticing him too. The parish council was happy to include Frederick when they needed leaflets delivering and as one thing leads to another, he became interested in local matters attending council meetings where he discovered that his family was not the only one with difficulties and that people were needed to speak for them.

A good-looking chap, it was inevitable that he should have admirers amongst the local girls both in chapel and at work in the vinery. But just as those early Cockaynes had been he was single-minded when it came to business. He might still be learning but with a clear idea where he was heading, lounging around after work with a crowd of young folks was not on his agenda. Nor did he have the money to spend on luxuries. Every penny was needed first for his mother, secondly to pay for his studies and if there was anything left it went into a building society for the deposit on his own vinery.

I have to remind myself that there were no teenagers in those days. Once you left school you were at work so the attitudes of young people were different from those of today.

***

It was around now that Frederick fell in love. She was the daughter of the local garage-owner at a time when only the rich and successful owned a car. But even while they courted Frederick made it perfectly clear where his priorities lay.

***

He was never a cruel man, indeed he was the kindest father in the world, but he knew what had to be done and would never have allowed his personal feelings to get in the way of his family commitments.

***

Poor Frederick. His love was short-lived. She was a sickly girl and finally succumbed to the illness that had plagued her all her life, but not before he had become interested in the religious sect to which she and her father belonged.

Alone again now and saddened by her loss he saw it as the reason for throwing himself wholeheartedly into what would help him achieve his ambitions.

***

Always the optimist he was a man who saw opportunities in difficulties. It was a maxim that was to serve him well in the years to come.

***

Was it the memory of his lost love that decided him to join The Plymouth Brethren? Whatever the reason he was to keep faith with it for the rest of his life and whilst maintaining his connection with the Methodists, more and more he realised that he preferred the Bible orientated thinking of the Brethren. Almost at once he became a lay preacher, finding comfort in the readings and preparation of the sermons.

When he met Ruth Catherine Mahy, it was not love at first sight. Indeed he was still too scarred by his first romantic experience to be anxious to try it again. He supposed she and her family had always been around the chapel, he simply hadn't noticed her. But when she did finally come into his orbit he was surprised by how much they had in common. She was attractive, modest not brash like a lot of the girls. Quiet and of good manners she was gently and kindly spoken with compassion and understanding. Instinctively he knew that she would have a high moral code, something that was important to him in his future wife.

They began to spend time together. She never asking him to be with her when he had other things to do, he beginning to rely on her for companionship and for understanding as he struggled to keep so many options on the road. It was a friendship that developed slowly at first and then into a relationship the like of which Frederick had never known before. One thing he finally knew was that he wanted to spend the rest of his life with this woman and that he would devote it to her happiness. From now on, although he never neglected his own family she would be the focus of all his endeavours.

In love he might be but Frederick was something his father had never been, he was a realist and he knew that whatever he might want to do for Ruth it would be impossible if he let love dictate the terms. If they were to be happy and successful then he had still much to achieve.

He was brutally honest. 'I want to marry you Ruth, but not until I can provide for you properly.'

It was scarcely the proposal for which she had been hoping.

For a long moment she just stared at him. There was a sincerity about this man that she had grown to love. She just knew he would never let her down and maybe that gleam in the dark eyes suggested he might be more in love with her than his recent declaration had suggested.

'Isn't there just something you might have omitted?' she was laughing now but he wasn't seeing it.

Overcome with embarrassment he muttered. 'I'm sorry. I love you Ruth. I just wanted to be fair to you.' He turned away.

Her arm stopped him. 'Don't I get to have a say in this?' She shook her head despairing at his clumsiness. 'Of course I'll marry you Frederick Cockayne,' she said. 'I love you.'

When he had finally got over the shock of her acceptance he explained how he saw their future. They must wait until he could buy his own vinery and provide a proper home for her.

Ruth knew it was not open to discussion. She either took him on those terms or not at all. There could be no compromise about something so fundamental to Frederick's thinking, so much a part of all that he had experienced.

It was a proposal not welcomed by Ruth's mother. Born into a wealthy, upper-class family and the product of an expensive education she may have had matrimonial ideas of a rather different nature for her daughter. The prospect of a serious wait before marriage suggested Frederick had a long way to go and perhaps she worried that having kept Ruth waiting there was still no guarantee he would marry her. It wouldn't be the first time that had happened. Was it that he just wasn't good enough, no proper education of the kind she understood and with the lowly ambition to have his own vinery? Scarcely a Rockefeller. Or was it that, as was common practice at the time, she had planned on keeping Ruth at home for her own needs and to take charge of domestic arrangements? Perhaps it was quite simply a case of "I do not like thee Doctor Fell" and as the rhyme goes "The reason why I cannot tell."

I was always conscious of the tension between my father and my grandmother. She came to tea once a fortnight on Sundays. The matriarch of the family she expected to be respected and obeyed. Whether she hoped to be loved I have no idea. I knew that I must always be on my best behaviour and I suppose I was a bit scared of her too. Now I think about it I suspect my father felt the same way. He was always anxious when she was expected, wanting everything to be just right and leaving no room for her criticism. But why? Surely by this time she had been convinced that her daughter had made not only a happy marriage but a prosperous one too for my father was now a highly respected member of the community, a successful business man owning several vineries exporting to different markets in the United Kingdom, with a beautiful home and luxury Ford car. My grandmother was a prominent salvationist with a string of achievements to her name so surely she could never have doubted that as a practising Christian he would have reneged on his word. To everyone else it seemed like a marriage made in heaven. And at that time there was nothing to suggest the tragedy which was to befall them.

✳✳✳

The wait was longer than either of them could have expected.

For Frederick it was part and parcel of his overall plan but for Ruth it was long and difficult and great credit to her that during that time she neither by look, word nor deed, showed her frustration.

In a world that seemed far away from their own gentle island, a war was brewing. The Kaiser, Queen Victoria's eldest grandson and deeply envious of his British cousin George V was eager to demonstrate his military and naval power and marched into Belgium. It was aggression not to be tolerated and within days the British government retaliated and war was declared.

YOUR COUNTRY NEEDS YOU

In every city and town, every village and hamlet the call was heard. The red-blooded youth of the country responded and queues formed outside recruiting offices. Brothers and friends joined up together. Whole villages lost their young men in days. Whilst even the women, bowled over by these waves of patriotism, stood by the roadside waving their men off believing that with the might of Great Britain behind them this would be a show of power that would shock the Germans into immediate surrender and the men would be home to celebrate Christmas.

In Guernsey news filtered through more slowly but the response was the same. Every able-bodied man of the right age presented himself at the Recruiting Office.

Frederick Charles Cockayne was one of the first.

✳✳✳

I find this difficult to believe considering how devoted he was to his family and especially his mother who must have still been relying on him at this time. And what about Ruth? What must she have thought? With what we know now about the progress of that war such action seems the height of folly.

✳✳✳

High on adrenalin, loyal to King and Country, and like the knights of old and those bowmen of Agincourt Frederick was aching to fight and burning with the romantic concept of war. Part of the first wave of British Expeditionary Forces he was in France almost before he had paraded his new uniform.

✳✳✳

This is a father I never knew, one who acted on impulse and, moved by stories of knights in shining armour, did something so out of character. Was he carried along on a wave of patriotism or was it possible that having had little or no childhood and huge responsibility during that time he longed to do something on the spur of the moment and the army presented him with just such a chance? For the first time in his life he was a free man. Plymouth Brethren accept the role of violence in society seeking and finding frequent references in the Bible to support this belief.

✳✳✳

The truth was very different.

And as he dug trenches and lived out of a mess tin with a fork and spoon, Guernsey became little more than a far-off memory.

12,000,000 troops from the Allied Powers. 1,700,000 dead.

Battle after battle over the Belgium port of Ypres, with Passchendaele one of the bloodiest and Frederick Charles Cockayne at the heart of it.

Sergeant Frederick Cockayne won his WW1 Campaign Medals. 1914 Star, British War Medal and Victory Medal, affectionately known as Pip, Squeak and Wilfred.

✳✳✳

"You ask what it is like. It's hell on earth. There's the scream of shells, the strange explosive sound of rifle fire like drawing corks from bottles, the regular tap, tap, tap of machine guns and all the time shrapnel raining down on trenches and fields.

But not twenty miles back from the Front there's a kind of peace even amongst the bombed-out villages and churches. The few locals who have stayed throughout it all share their wine with us and make us the odd meal with what meat and vegetables they can find. But it's the quietness that strikes you the most. Your ears have learned to accept that sounds of war are the norm and the quietness becomes nearly as frightening as the relentless shelling.

And despite all the ruins, all the fighting, flowers and plants still find a way to flourish and the birds sing.

When you're in the midst of it you long for Rest and Rehabilitation. But after a couple of days all you can think about is being back, seeing your mates and getting stuck in." Tipperary

✳✳✳

So why did I never ask about it? I suppose because I was too young and because by the time I came along it was never mentioned so I wasn't even curious. I remember seeing distinctive blue uniforms and being told they were wounded soldiers and of being a bit frightened of angry looking men with crippled limbs as they staggered about on rough wooden crutches. Today we understand post-traumatic stress but in those days it was stiff-upper lip. Men didn't cry nor did they share that kind of information even with their wives. So I wonder what life would have been like for both my father and my mother in those post war years. How did my father slot back into life on a tiny island? How do you make love when you've seen the horror of the trenches, your friends and comrades blown to pieces and at the command of a whistle gone over the top? Because my father was the kind of man he was I imagine that he would keep his memories private and concentrate on making a good life for himself and my mother.

✳✳✳

When he finally came home there was only one thing for Frederick to do. He must throw himself into the business. There were years to make up both to himself and more especially to Ruth who had waited at home for his return. And if you needed therapy, which Frederick must have done, where better than the peace and quiet of a vinery, the loudest noise that of the steam engine when it came to sterilise the soil. For days he buried himself in his work, rising at dawn and making straight for the greenhouse and only going home when it was dusk and he was physically too exhausted to do more than crawl into bed. That he awoke sometimes shouting and covered in sweat was never mentioned. The belief being that it would be too embarrassing for everybody concerned.

With Ruth's encouragement he rented a small vinery and entered the world of business for himself. Well-trained he knew how to grow tomatoes that would soon be recognised for taste and quality. Searching for the right market was a challenge he enjoyed. But alongside this was his determination to find a home. It was seven years to the day since his proposal when he finally walked Ruth down the small chapel aisle. A cottage had become vacant near the vinery and although it was rented it was a beginning and Frederick was confident that it was only a matter of time before he embarked on the building of a house that would be to their design and belong to them.

It was a wish echoed by Ruth who deposited her posy of flowers as an offering to La Gran'mère du Chimquière, making a silent prayer that she would bring them luck in the years ahead. It was scarcely the action of a devout Christian but it was her wedding day and a bit of luck was surely permissible. Frederick seemed to think so too when he swung her into his arms and carried her across the threshold of their tiny cottage.

The years that followed were much like most people's, a mixture of the good and the bad. The good was all about Frederick's business going from strength to strength with orders pouring in and Frederick producing more tomatoes to satisfy the needs of his customers. Sometimes Ruth helped when an extra pair of hands was required but for the most part it was down to Frederick. The bad was their health. Probably due to his experiences in the trenches Frederick developed a respiratory condition which resulted in the loss of a lung. Ruth's problem involved them both. More than anything they longed for a child, the natural outpouring of their love for each other. But as the years passed it became clear that there would be no children and when eventually Ruth had a hysterectomy they knew they must give up all hope. It was a bitter pill but what concerned Frederick even more than the dashing of their hopes was that Ruth was no longer a well woman and he knew that now he must stop mourning the loss of a future family and concentrate his attention on the woman he loved.

✳✳✳

And love her he did. People were not so demonstrative in those days but even though I was only a child I would see the way he looked for her as soon as he walked in and how he would take her hand and just for a moment it was as if I wasn't there.

✳✳✳

The word good is used often without regard to its true meaning but the Cockaynes, Ruth and Frederick were good people. They loved their fellow man but they did it with such humility that no one ever felt patronised. For them religion was all embracing and had little to do with attending service, although they were regular chapel goers. It was so much more than paying lip-service to God, it was about doing the best you could and thinking it a privilege. Friends and neighbours sought their advice and sometimes just came to unburden themselves. No one was ever turned away.

And as Frederick's business empire grew so too did his standing on the island. He was a respected member of the business community known for helping those at the top who had overstretched themselves and those at the bottom who hardly knew where to begin. He believed that growth in business was about individual success becoming part of a larger co-operative enterprise.

From now on Cockayne progress was steady as one vinery followed another, occupying more and more acres of land. And finally a field of daffodils, something he had promised himself all those years back at night school. Now though with no prospect of ever having a family Ruth became more and more involved in the running of the business. Their logo, FRCM (Frederick Ruth Cockayne Mahy) was well known in business circles in Guernsey and in England and France.

One of my earliest recollections is of a "host of golden daffodils fluttering and dancing in the breeze" and of my father bringing me a handful of tiny flowers. And there's another memory, lying in a bunk with my mother, struggling to find the room to curl up alongside her, desperate to share the warmth of her body and her saying, 'Let's stop thinking about how hungry and cold we are and think of something lovely. Something beautiful that we remember.' And then our hearts with pleasure filled and danced with the Guernsey daffodils.

❋❋❋

From now on the Cockayne empire, just like the days of the emporium, was set to expand. Tomatoes and daffodils provided a busy trade with the markets of Bristol and Covent Garden. Six vineries of 2,000 feet and three fields of daffodils provided not just for Frederick but for a small army of people who worked for him.

There was one thing still missing from their paradise, a child and as now there was no prospect of that ever happening Frederick concentrated on the one thing he could do for his wife. He would build her the promised house. Ideally along a steep, narrow lane next to the greenhouses there was a plot of land more than enough for building and with plenty to spare for an orchard and small holding. It was a project that would keep them both busy and especially Ruth who needed something positive on which to focus her attention.

He and Ruth explained exactly what they wanted from the architect. It was what we would now call a chalet bungalow. They employed the finest builders. The kitchen had to be the latest in technology, though being the early 1930s what was top of the range then bears no resemblance to today. However the final touch which made every neighbour sit up and take note, they installed a bathroom and lavatory. At a time when there was no main drainage most people still used an outside privy and drew water from a pump. A cesspit located some little distance from the bungalow was the answer. The day it was complete Frederick took Ruth to France in search of antique furniture which would add character and craftsmanship to their new home. And when all was done there was Frederick's gift to Ruth. A baby grand piano. She was a fine musician and he was sure that the instrument would be a solace and comfort.

***

Of course, I knew none of this. Even so I recall her playing and my dancing to a Chopin Polonaise. I remember too how my father and I gathered round the piano to sing hymns, his deep voice blending strangely with mine.

***

And then out of the blue something happened that was to turn their lives around forever. They heard of a child who needed them as much as they needed her.

It was a sad story. A baby had been born to a woman on her deathbed. The father, an itinerant musician, already had a large family and no desire to add to it. In practical terms he couldn't cope with the care of an existing family never mind a tiny baby. Financially there was only so much money in the pot and that was already spoken for. Emotionally he had no affection for a child that had cost him the life of his wife and had robbed his children of their mother. One way or another she would have to go somewhere else. Foster home or institution. And then someone mentioned adoption.

It was the perfect solution. The man was pleased to have an option which would hopefully be the best for the child, would stop his feeling guilty about the arrangement and with a bit of luck could be enacted speedily.

On an island news travels fast. A friend of the Cockaynes heard the story and contacted Frederick immediately. Adoption had never been in their minds, maybe the hurt was still too raw or was it that they wondered if they were too old to begin the process. But this would be a private arrangement, no agencies involved. Even so, Frederick was anxious not to raise Ruth's hopes, so he decided to see the man and the child for himself without telling her.

It was a modest little cottage and there seemed to be children everywhere, some playing games others looking as if they didn't know what to do. Frederick's heart went out to them. And because he saw the hurt he knew he had to be very sure that this was what the man really wanted and not something he would regret. The child was sleeping wrapped up and resting in a drawer. 'May I hold her?' The man lifted the baby and placed her in Frederick's arms. Just at that moment two tiny eyes peered up at him. As he said later to Ruth, 'That was it. My heart went out to her.' But he insisted on seeing the child properly. If there were physical problems then he had to make sure Ruth understood exactly what they were taking on.

'I shall need my wife to see her and be happy with the idea.'

The man looked uncertain. He needed action now not in a few days.

'Today,' Frederick reassured him, 'and there is something else, the adoption will be final. No going back and to that end I will require an advocate to draw up legal papers to be signed by us both and only at that point would I consider the adoption binding and take the child. I have a friend who could move the matter on within days for us. Do you agree?'

Now he hurried home to break the news to Ruth praying that she would feel just as he had done and that when she saw the little girl she would want her in the same way he had.

Ruth listened to him in silence and then burst into tears.

'I'm so sorry, my love I thought it might be the answer but only if you want it.'

'It's the most wonderful thing that has happened. When can I see her?'

She cried again when she saw the tiny creature sleeping in the blanket-lined drawer. 'May I hold her?'

When she was seated and the baby in her arms, the two men by mutual consent walked away. There were matters to discuss and neither wanted to witness the depth of Ruth's emotion as she rocked the longed for child close to her breast. But when she asked if she could take her home right away it was Frederick who refused.

'When Margaret comes to us and I promise it will be soon, my dear, it must be legally binding. She must be ours for all time and,' he indicated the other man, 'Margaret's father must relinquish all connections or claims to her. I have an advocate who is waiting to draw up the papers and once they are signed by him and by me, then we may have our dear little girl.'

Ruth's pleas were in vain. On an emotional level Frederick wanted Margaret out of that house at once, but he was not a successful businessman for nothing. He knew that human nature can play tricks and that promises and reassurances do not always lead to a satisfactory conclusion. And although he said nothing of this to Ruth he acknowledged that when it came to signing away his daughter the man might not be able to go through with it. For himself the whole idea was unthinkable.

***

My father could never have given up a child, even if he had a house full and no money. I remember him once commenting on Jane Austen's family and how they gave up one of their sons to some wealthy cousins to be adopted, and brought up and educated as theirs. And of course the whole attitude to children was so different. Families were huge, eight or nine children being common with several deaths at birth. But this was the 1930s and although there were several children in the family it was nothing like the numbers in Georgian times. When I think about it, and that's not often, I make some excuse for the fact that my birth father was grieving for his dead wife and may have felt a sense of duty to his existing children rather than a new one. That he might have resented me is also a possibility. After all it was my arrival that had robbed him of his wife, the mother of his children, the woman he needed to keep the family afloat.

***

A child is born. And whilst Ruth hadn't experienced the traumas of birth, in every other respect there was no difference in what was to follow. Once the paperwork was complete Ruth, wheeling a brand-new pram, went with Frederick to collect their daughter. For them an emotionally charged moment. For the man seeing them off relief.

Neighbours had looked after the child up to then so he had known no affection and experienced no feelings of loss. And as far as he was concerned there is no suggestion that was ever to change.

***

Years were to pass, indeed I was wheeling my own child in a pram when I was suddenly accosted in the street by a woman claiming that I was part of her family, indeed a sister. I was shocked and horrified, almost scared. 'I have a family,' I told her,' and want no other.' From birth I had known of my adoption and it had never been an issue until that moment. I ran home where my father dug out the signed and dated adoption papers assuring me that I need never have anything to do with these people. They made a couple more attempts but I was having none of it and have never regretted it. I am a Cockayne, brought up as one and never thinking of myself as anything else.

***

The next few years were to be the happiest the Cockayne family would ever know. Frederick and Ruth had a child and unlike many adopted children she came with no preconceived ideas, attitudes or manners. She was theirs to mould as they thought fit. The Cockaynes would write her story and they would write it almost from birth.

Halcyon Days. A new baby "mewling and puking" was a delight. Sleepless nights were what you expected. Choosing the right food, the best bottle, the most comfortable clothes were all a pleasure. These were not people in their first youth, they were a mature couple welcoming the challenge of parenthood.

Love is love wherever you find it but Margaret was especially fortunate, the love that enveloped her was gold-wrapped. The

Cockaynes had land, vineries, daffodil fields and money, plenty of it. Frederick's dream had finally come true.

***

And if I had been able to dream as a baby I could not have wished for anything more. I had been adopted by a family able to not just provide for my every need but to do it with style, panache and love. There was nothing too good for me. Only one thing remained that was to prove impossible for those generous kind-hearted parents. I wanted a brother. I had seen them about. Other people had them. I had cousins but that wasn't the same. Their brothers lived with them in the same house. They looked after some of the younger ones, well when they were in the mood. I knew where to go to get one. My parents were always telling me to take my troubles to God. Well I did. Every evening with my parents kneeling by my bedside I would speak to God.

'Please God send me a brother,' and to make it easier for him I would add, 'an older brother.'

Needless to say God had difficulties with this particular request and, as my dear old-fashioned parents were never likely to explain, the matter lay unresolved while they trotted out lame excuses that God has his own plans and he sees the bigger picture for everybody.

***

They were indulgent, protective parents but Margaret was never spoiled. While Frederick worked in his business, Ruth devoted herself to bringing up and educating their little daughter. It was a labour of love as Ruth instilled good manners, kindness and compassion while even, gentle discipline was all part of the overall plan for their child's good.

***

My mother was the gentlest of women. I never remember her raising her voice in anger but if she told you to do something you never argued but straight away obeyed. I've often wondered just how she did it. Was there a look in the eyes or a slight change of speech? Whatever it was it always worked and I see now how much that must have helped me in the years that were to come.

I remember a bitter lesson the memory of which was to last me all my life. I could see Uncle Bertie approaching the house carrying a box wrapped up in special paper. It was so unusual for us to give or receive presents I was overcome with anticipation and incapable of speech. 'What do you say?' prompted my mother. I heard her without hearing her or understanding, all I wanted to do was open it and I scrabbled away at the wrappings. It was the most beautiful thing I had ever seen and I could scarcely believe it was for me, a dolls' tea-set displayed piece by piece in a pretty box. 'What do you say?' prompted my mother. Again I heard without hearing and she removed the box from my hand, wrapped it up and sadly gave it back to Uncle Bertie, 'I'm sure you can find some little girl who will appreciate this gift better than Margaret.' I can still feel the shock and hurt but I have never forgotten my thanks since.

***

They played together, the mother and daughter. They recited nursery rhymes and sang songs. They walked down to the beach where Ruth would hire a chair and watch Margaret building sandcastles and searching for shells and coloured pebbles. And as soon as she was old enough they went shopping, buying pretty dresses and beautiful shoes. An indulgent Frederick delighting in watching a Ruth who bloomed in her newly found happiness and he never tired of the way Margaret wrapped her arms around him, as she looked for the warmth of his hug.

School was a hurdle for Ruth. She hated the idea of her tiny child going off to school where she would meet rough children and learn behaviour that Ruth would prefer she didn't. To minimise the extent of this influence Ruth took and collected Margaret from school. And there was something else too, the fact that her father was Plymouth Brethren must have been another concern for her knowing as she did that Frederick had completely different ideas from those of other parents at Margaret's school.

It was about now that Frederick changed his car and bought a Ford Model A Roadster.

✳✳✳

I loved this car with its running boards, gold trimmings and tassels and picnic basket on the back. Now when my father went to do business with overseas buyers he would take Mama and me. We would drive down to the harbour and a huge crane would pick up the car and swing it over the side of the boat and onto the deck. Then we would go into the First Class Saloon for the journey while the boat tossed and turned its way across the Channel. Not many people left the island in those days so everybody noticed and wanted to know all about it when we got back. In 1935 Mama learned to drive and took the driving test which had just come into force. The hill start was then as it is today, a challenge for many people. Once the car was halted on a slope the examiner would get out and place a matchbox behind the back wheel. If you crushed it when you restarted the car it was an automatic failure. Dada and I were so proud when Mama passed first time. Uncle Gershom had a car with a peep peep town horn and a loud klaxon country horn. He would drive with me between his knees and let me sound the country horn.

✳✳✳

Bristol was a favourite place and Frederick had good business contacts there. He'd book a hotel and Ruth and Margaret would explore the city and smart shops. It was a heady experience for a tiny girl. She became used to staying at the best hotels and being waited upon. She enjoyed meeting people and because of the nature of her parents she learned to be quietly appreciative and value the service of others, and so wherever she went people warmed to this little girl.

✳✳✳

We would drive over the Clifton Suspension Bridge and my father would point out the Latin inscription SUSPENSA VIX VIA FIT which means a suspended way made with difficulty. For him the story of the twenty three year old Brunel embarking on a project which would take thirty three years and was only completed after his death signified that there was nothing you could not achieve if you believed in it strongly enough and were prepared to put in the work. I just loved the strange feel as the car rattled across and enjoyed the excitement of a strong wind taking the car and moving it momentarily across the bridge.

Much as it had been in the early 19th century, religion played a big part in the Cockayne household. On Sunday, wearing the clothes they kept for weddings and funerals, everybody attended chapel. In the evening Frederick often preached at the Plymouth Brethren Meeting Hall. It was a day of reflection, a day when, as God had dictated, he rested.

But there were lots of other days when the Cockaynes worked and played hard too. Because of his standing in the community Frederick and his family were invited to any kind of celebration or special occasion on the island. If the Bailiff gave a soiree or party the Cockaynes were there. When the Royal Guernsey Militia held any sort of event or garden party the family were there. With an eight-hundred-year-old history of unpaid volunteers defending the island it was only natural that it should have much to celebrate. Known as the Guernsey Light Infantry, from 1916 to 1919 its war honours included Ypres, Passchendaele and Cambrai. All part of Frederick's war years.

✳✳✳

I loved those parties, wearing my prettiest dress and always being taken to meet the regimental goat, resplendent in his fine coat and decorations. It's only years later that I see this as a contradiction in terms. How was it possible for us to share public celebrations or parties when Dad's religion forbade him to do so even in the confines of his own home. Or was it that these events were linked to battle honours and akin to Plymouth Brethren thinking?

✳✳✳

Such wonderful days for the Cockayne family were not repeated around the globe.

These were "The Thirties". Humanity's darkest, bloodiest time. Mass poverty, extremism and growing rumours that the war that was supposed to have ended all wars was likely to be followed by another very soon. The Wall Street Crash marked the beginning of global economic depression. In the United Kingdom stagnation in the 1920s lead to the Depression of the Thirties, high unemployment and mass poverty. Two hundred men set off from Jarrow in Tyneside to march to London to petition the government to reinstate a shipbuilding industry that had collapsed.

It was inevitable that unemployment and poverty on this scale would lead to the rise of extremism. Governments had failed the people and in their desperation they were looking for answers, any answers from whatever source, Hitler and Nazism, Goebbels and his Brownshirts and Mussolini and his Blackshirts.

The outcome, 60 million dead and the industrial slaughter of 6 million Jews.

In Europe Germany was the worst affected. The United States called in the loans which had been the basis for the Weimar reparations demanded by the Allies after WW1. As the loans were removed industry collapsed and Germany sank into The Depression.

By the time Hitler came to power one in three Germans was unemployed and had lost all faith in democracy. Hungry, unemployed and desperate they were ready to listen to the manipulative public speaking of anybody and any solutions they might have. It was the world's disaster that the man who fired their imaginations be Adolf Hitler who attributed the world's problems to the Jews.

It is also true that because governments had so many problems of their own they failed to realise the extent of Hitler's influence or were just unwilling to face facts. Agents and travellers reported what they had seen and heard in Germany but few people were taking notice and by the time they did it was too late. The battle lines were drawn and it was going to be five cruel years before the lights would go back on in Europe.

And what of Frederick at this time? Living on an island protects you a little from the rest of the world. And this was the thirties when communication was very different. But even had it been better how many people would have voiced fears? How many people truly believed that so few years after WW1 there would be another major conflict? Even Guernsey's economic depression was managed as the Bailiwick quickly seized the opportunity to get some essential work done. Unemployed labourers were given jobs building sea defences and constructing roads. As for Frederick, trade between Guernsey and England continued much the same as before. The people who had bought the tomatoes and the daffodils in the past were still buying them. Wooden trays became chip baskets to transport tomatoes. Ruth and Margaret still accompanied Frederick on his business trips to Bristol.

***

Did my Father shut his mind to the rumours that floated around? Surely when he attended meetings with the Bailiff and events at the barracks the topic must have come up? Was it that he believed that whatever happened it would not involve him or his little island? Did he, like so many others, believe it couldn't, wouldn't happen again?

Was it possible that he did heed the warnings but took care never to speak of these concerns in front of me?

***

An estranged Churchill warned of an imminent threat, but he had no voice in a government peopled by the likes of the peace appeaser Neville Chamberlain.

By 1939 some of the newspaper stories were beginning to be believed. They were certainly believed when they reported the forced surrender of Czechoslovakia and Austria. It was the beginning of Hitler's plan to bring German speaking people together and for that he needed *Lebensraum* or living space. And where better than Poland, a large country with an abundance of agricultural land. It was the threat to Poland that finally convinced the British Government of Hitler's intended aggression and forced them to issue a warning.

In Guernsey military and police guards were mounted on key installations.

German tanks rolled across the Polish border in the early hours of September 1st.

At 9.am on the morning of September 3rd Neville Henderson, Britain's Ambassador to Germany issued an ultimatum stating that if hostilities did not end by 11am a state of war would exist between Great Britain and Germany.

With no response from Germany by 11.15 the Prime Minister Neville Chamberlain went on radio and announced that the British people were at war with Germany.

***

I have no real recollection of this. I remember my parents listening to the radio and speaking quietly together afterwards. But as always in anything that might give me concern they were careful to monitor their own reactions. Next day I heard a garbled version of the truth from other children whose parents had made no effort to protect them from the dreadful news. In the playground rumours were passed round with great glee and eager anticipation of what was to come. Small boys leapt around with everybody wanting to be British and nobody prepared to be the enemy.

✳✳✳

Amongst the adult population there was shock but also a conviction that it wouldn't affect them. The idea that Germany would invade never crossed their minds. In any case these were men with genes still strong with the will and need to fight. For centuries the Bailiwick had exploited its closeness to mainland Europe by applying for letters of marque, licenses that allowed the fitting out and arming of vessels to be used in the capture of enemy merchant shipping in a way which would otherwise have been deemed piracy. They sailed the seas and built navies, manning them with local men used to the vagaries of the turbulent oceans. Such was their prowess that they earned the admiration and respect of Horatio Nelson. They fought and held their corner in the worst days of WW1.

These were not men likely to be intimidated by the likes of Adolf Hitler or a country it had well and truly defeated once and would do so again.

However, Frederick and his brother Jack did not share the wave of patriotism that swept the island. For them this was a time of reflection, remembering the wave of enthusiasm that had sent them off down the recruiting office once before, convinced that they would give the Germans what for and be home by Christmas.

The truth had been rather different. Hand to hand fighting, bloodshed and lives slaughtered on a scale that thankfully would never be repeated. And at the end a treaty drawn up that would destroy a country already devastated by war, starvation and poverty. Although Frederick and Jack had no reason to love the Germans they knew enough about them to know that robbing them of everything might not have been the best answer at the end of WW1. And it was this knowledge that made Frederick angry. Hadn't they endured the trenches and the loss of their pals only to have politicians make a mess of the peace and lead them to where they were facing yet another war.

Even so as they talked neither thought for a moment that they would be asked to serve. Too old and in Frederick's case no longer fit.

Although my parents were reluctant to talk about the war, we all had to abide by new regulations and it was important that I should understand them too. Even on the first day police came round shouting 'Put those lights out.' As we were only burning candles it seemed a bit unreasonable but my father explained that any light would be visible from the air and we didn't want to help the enemy. Next morning my mother rushed off to buy material for blackout curtains. Cinemas and theatres were closed. Cars were reduced to 15mph and side lights.

***

There was no conscription although some Guerns, anxious to be part of the conflict from the beginning, crossed the Channel to volunteer. More than one thousand joined up in the first four months.

But after the initial response life on the island returned almost to normal. People continued with their jobs. The vineries operated as usual, trade visits were still being made across the Channel and wealthy visitors were coming to the island to get away from the increasing doom and gloom at home, although after two weeks of closure the government had to reopen places of entertainment because of the low morale amongst the public. Even the passports and permit cards which had been introduced at the beginning of the war were abolished.

People were wondering what the fuss had been about and were talking of a phoney war.

It was the invasion of Denmark and Norway that made some islanders begin to feel less comfortable.

The Germans were moving rapidly now and the Maginot Line which was said to be the work of a genius, impervious to aerial bombings and tank fire, was by-passed when the Germans used the Ardennes Forest to secure their hold in France and bring about the evacuation of Dunkirk. The invasion of Holland, Belgium and Luxembourg made islanders sit up and take notice. Guernsey's tiny airport became the launching pad for Operation Haddock when thirty-six Whitley bombers attacked Turin and Genoa. The war that had seemed so far away was suddenly on their doorstep.

Regulations which had been relaxed during the Phoney War were reintroduced, all major installations were under armed guard, German nationals residing on the island were deported to England for the duration of the war as much for their own safety as for the likelihood of their being spies. Local feeling was running high and anyone of German or Austrian origin and later Italian was deeply suspect.

✳✳✳

I remember my father being distressed by the deportation of a friend even while acknowledging it was probably for the best.

✳✳✳

It was the fall of Paris that upset people the most. If the French and the British hadn't managed to save Paris what hope had they? Islanders spent the weekend down at the harbour trying to decide whether to just leave and hop on the next boat.

But it was the fall of Dunkirk that changed everything. A destroyed British Army was ferried back across the Channel in small boats and now the military in Guernsey was about to follow suit.

✳✳✳

My father and mother seemed always to be talking together, my mother anxious whenever she thought I wasn't looking and my father more serious than I had ever seen him trying to comfort and reassure her.

✳✳✳

Within days the news that nobody had expected. The Channel Isles were to be demilitarized. A saddened Churchill announced that Guernsey would become an open town, the Militia would surrender all uniforms and weapons and all guns must be handed in. The oldest most valued possession of the Crown would be taken over without a shot being fired on its behalf. For reasons of security this information was not forwarded to the Germans who wrongly believed that Guernsey would be defended and launched a preliminary attack.

On the island boats were commandeered from yacht clubs and the garrison was ordered to leave immediately even while they were eating lunch.

***

Although I still didn't understand a lot that was happening I knew something was seriously wrong. I could hear my mother weeping and my father and his brother Jack spending a long time talking, a conversation my mother said I was not to interrupt.

***

One of the characteristics of Guernsey people is their ability to face life as it comes, look at problems without unnecessary emotion and do what needs to be done. But for some everything was happening too swiftly. From living on an island protected by the military, almost overnight it was undefended. They didn't have the time to be angry. For some that came later. Many were just too frightened. The Bailiff, on the orders of the British Government, urged the people to stand firm and continue as before. Statesmen and people in authority were going to stay. Somebody had to continue to run the country. Frederick Cockayne amongst them.

The question of whether the United Kingdom was right to leave the island undefended has been the subject of many arguments and raised questions. To some it seemed like a betrayal of centuries of loyalty to the Crown for it not to come to their aid. Being robbed of the chance to fight for itself was a bitter pill.

My father despite everything that was to happen to him, saw the bigger picture and as he was to explain to me later, Britain was ill prepared for war in 1939. It had neither trained men nor the arms needed to fight a major conflict. If Hitler had had any idea of the true situation he would have followed up the defeat of Dunkirk, crossed the Channel, destroying the Channel Islands on the way and invaded England. Instead he turned his attention elsewhere giving Britain time. The Battle of France was lost and defending the Channel Isles would have required military power Britain simply didn't have. And the advantage to Hitler's invading the Channel Isles was no more than useful propaganda. German boots on British soil. Guernsey would be sacrificed for the greater good.

✳✳✳

Newspapers announced the evacuation of children, teachers and mothers with young children under school age. Decisions had to be made at once and applications registered. Anybody who wanted to leave must register to do so and men of military age still on the island were urged to evacuate.

On the 20th June the last troop ship left together with some French citizens.

The effect on the public was devastating. Even those who had still been saying nothing despaired. Now they knew what it was like to be isolated and rejected by those they had always believed cared. Nobody knew what to do. 'Are you going? Are you staying?' People rushed around asking friends and family and hoping somebody might have positive answers to help their decision.

Beyond the Wire

For many islanders sailing to the nearby island of Sark was an adventure. The idea that they or their dearest would be crossing the Channel was too much to contemplate.

***

The strange thing was that during this terrible period of uncertainty the export of island produce continued. English people departed. A third of the growers left even with two fifths of their crops still on the plants. Some farmers slaughtered their cattle but most elected to stay. Some growers carried on sending flowers and potatoes to market until ordered to stop and on one day alone 350,000 chips of tomatoes were shipped to the United Kingdom. So, my father still believed he had a business to run and presumably that he had nothing to fear whatever happened. Certainly he never contemplated leaving the island although he urged my mother to take me. 'I must keep the business going.' He told her.

Her reply was positive. 'We're a family. We all stay or we all go. Margaret isn't going alone. I'm not going without you and if you won't go then we shall all stay.' It was something about which she would never voice regret despite everything that happened.

Surely, surely if Dada had really understood his position he would never have taken the chance and put us all at risk by staying.

***

The truth is that Frederick Charles Cockayne, born in Ireland to a Guernsey woman and an English soldier regarded himself a Guern. It never crossed his mind that officialdom would see him as anything else. Hadn't he spent nearly his entire life on the island. He certainly had no real recollection of being anywhere else. This was a man passionately devoted to his wife and little daughter and when they decided to stay with him despite his begging them to evacuate he must have thought that they and he were at absolutely no risk.

All around them people prepared to say goodbye to their loved ones for the duration of a war which looked increasingly likely to be a long one. For some of the evacuees they entered a life much more luxurious than the peasant one they had experienced in Guernsey and which made their eventual return to the island fraught with difficulties. For others they became cheap labour and there were many who knew no love or affection from their hosts just ill-concealed annoyance at the government's audacity in forcing them to house evacuees. But there were just as many who were welcomed into families forging relationships that would last for the rest of their lives. Contact with home was via the Red Cross, with censored messages of no more than 25 words. Just about enough space to say I'm well. What none of their families anticipated was that they might never see their children again or that some might return only to go back to the United Kingdom where they had grown up and now felt more comfortable.

This was a civilian evacuation with none of the planning of a military exercise. There was confusion and misunderstanding of what they were to do. Half the population wanted to leave. 80 percent of children of school age were registered. There was a run on the bank, shops ran out of suitcases while mothers tried to equip their children with the basics they would need in their new homes, nobody wanting their children to be disadvantaged. A list was provided; gas masks, ration books, overcoat or mackintosh, a change of clothing, boots, shoes, plimsolls, night clothes and toiletries. Sandwiches egg or cheese, nuts, raisins, biscuits, barley sugar, apple and orange were provided for the journey. Some children were simply given a dozen hard-boiled eggs.

Because of the threat of air raids people were not allowed to say goodbye to their children on the quay but must do so either at home or in the school assembly point.

***

I was too young to appreciate the drama being enacted around me but looking back now I begin to understand the anguish of those parents and the fears of children suddenly uprooted from loving families. Imagine seeing your children going to a far-off land sailing across a stretch of water open to attack from sea and air to live with people forced to give them a roof over their heads.

***

What was abundantly clear was that more people wanted to go than were able to find places on the boats and there was a steady stream of families who returned to their homes dragging their hastily packed suitcases behind them. Some had already shot their family pets. Growers had left their precious crops exposed to the elements with greenhouse doors and vents left open. Cars had been sold for as little as one pound.

***

As the last boats left we stayed at home, politely leaving these unhappy people to sort out their shattered lives and come to terms with the loss of their children or the fact that they were forced to stay on an island about to be occupied. It was now that I saw my first enemy plane. A reconnaissance flew slowly over the island taking photographs. I could see the black cross on the fuselage and wings. I could even see the pilot in his cockpit. I ran inside frightened by its closeness and wondering what he meant to do. The word went out that the Germans would be landing soon and that they were to be treated courteously and no resistance offered.

✳✳✳

With the boats taking most of the children gone there settled an unreal stillness on the island. Not unlike Hamelin when the Pied Piper took the children away.

It was the silence of waiting.

They didn't have long to wait, for three planes flew in along the harbour wall where a group of small children, who had never intended to leave or had been left behind after the last boat sailed now waved and jumped about excitedly. Their shouts of welcome were lost as the bombs fell on what were thought to be military lorries but were in fact farm trucks with men unloading tomatoes ready for the next boat to ferry them to the United Kingdom.

✳✳✳

The air raid sounded and my father told my mother and me to get under the bed. We could hear the planes going over and the sound of the bombing. I remember trembling all over and Mama holding me close and playing a game of pretty pictures. I had to think of something nice and describe it and then Mama would think of one. Once or twice though the sound was so loud that we were both too frightened to do anything except put our hands over our ears. When the all clear sounded my father helped us out and he tried to make light of it, but young though I was, I sensed that something had upset him deeply. Later he told my mother of the slaughter of innocent people, tomato growers like himself who had been blown to pieces.

***

33 dead. 67 injured. 49 vehicles burnt out. Bomb craters. Weighbridge damaged. The clock stopped.

An open town? An invasion without a shot being fired? How could this have happened?

The government had reassured that there need be no fear of Germany taking any advantage from the British decision to demilitarise the Channel Isles.

It later emerged that the decision to demilitarise had never been passed to Germany and had been suppressed on grounds that it gave away too much information. It was 30th June before it finally reached German High Command, by which time it was too late to save the island.

The following day an enemy plane flew over, clearly assessing the damage done by the raid and how much resistance the occupying forces were likely to meet.

Later that day a cargo of pigs left with four civilians who just as the boat was leaving leapt aboard in a last attempt to escape before the Germans arrived.

***

I don't think I shall ever really understand what my father hoped to gain by staying. The policy had been that women with young children would leave first. My father had money. He could easily have paid for us all to get out long before the panic evacuation started. Did he think he could save his business? He was a grower of tomatoes and daffodils, needing the services of a regular market to sell his goods. He was never going to be allowed to continue trading throughout the war and certainly not once we had been occupied. Was it that he hoped to look after his greenhouses and his home for the duration? Was it that he saw leaving as some sort of cowardice?

✳✳✳

On the 30th June at seven in the evening a Junkers 52 landed at the small airport with a platoon of Luftwaffe troops. Rumours of German brutality had swept across the island and as the plane came down some people ran out of their homes to hide. Women, believing the tales they had heard about German atrocities, refused to leave their homes for days. Others stood by the wayside, an unsmiling silent reception party. One or two women knelt in the road invoking the Clameur de Haro.

Haro. Haro. Haro.

A'laide mon prince

Come to my aid

My prince

Followed by the Lord's Prayer said in Guernsey French.

A prayer that even to this day can stop Guernsey people committing all kinds of offenses against their neighbours provided the transgressor witnesses the prayer and the law upholds the accusation.

In 1940 such a prayer was unlikely to have any effect on the German army but no doubt it gave the petitioner some satisfaction.

Beyond the Wire

And so the occupation began. Frederick joined islanders in St. Peter Port trying to find out the terms, if there were any. Huge posters appeared on every corner.

Curfew 11pm -6am

Airport out of bounds.

All traffic between islands forbidden.

No private cars or buses.

No petrol to be sold.

All cars to drive on right side of road.

Half the tomato crop to be destroyed and fed to cattle.

Bread available Tuesday, Thursday, Saturday.

Stocks of seeds requisitioned.

All spirits to be locked away and none sold.

Meat, Butter, Bacon, Sugar, Tea, Coffee, Cocoa and Salt rationed.

Tuesday and Friday meat free days.

Sale of candles prohibited.

A hundred weight of coal per week per house.

All bulb fields to be ploughed.

Cinemas closed two days a week to save electricity.

A reward for those who informed on islanders painting V for Victory signs on walls and buildings.

Plundering of evacuated property carried the death penalty.

And this was only the beginning as week succeeded week new restrictions were issued.

More rationing. Wireless sets confiscated.

Telephones disconnected.

Even the activities of the Salvation Army were suppressed.

Immediately the Germans began the construction of huge fortifications along the coast while inland they destroyed vineries and fields to dig out machine-gun posts and house the largest heavy guns. It was only after the war that the Islanders fully understood the extent of the destruction. Prevented from moving about they were unable to see that Guernsey, on the orders of Hitler, was being turned into an impregnable fortress. Convinced that Britain would launch an attack to retake the island Hitler threw everything he could at the fortification. With an unlimited budget, concrete, steel, finest engineering, tanks, soldiers were destined for the stronghold that would become Guernsey. Using triangulation and Freyer Radar to determine the enemy position, attacks from land, sea or air would be impossible without the full might of Germany's long-distanced guns being trained upon them. And as the war progressed the island became the centre for communication, passing information directly to and from Berlin using Enigma. And so that the fortress could continue to operate regardless of what was happening, there began the underground construction of 29 tunnels creating a military camp that would house men and machinery and with independent power would cater below ground for their every need. Hitler's Island madness was never known to the Allies until after the war but such was the quality of the building and design that even today many of the structures remain a lasting reminder.

Frederick's land was one of the first to go. Within hours the work of a lifetime had been turned into a pile of wood, glass and rotting tomatoes while great piles of bulbs lay waiting to be collected and destroyed. The land for which he had saved and worked so hard was taken from him in less than a day and turned into ditches and bunkers with anti-aircraft guns on his doorstep. It had become a tool in the hands of the enemy to bring down his own country.

✱✱✱

I remember my mother taking my father into her arms and their standing close together holding each other tight and how I ran up to them hugging them both, anxious to take part in whatever it was that was happening. Looking back I wonder if, like any small child, I might have found some of it exciting or was I frightened by their unhappiness and a feeling of insecurity? Suddenly right behind and close to our house were lots of soldiers and slave labour digging out holes and building huge cement blocks to house wooden structures to hold anti-aircraft guns. All my father's work lay in ruins, with mounds of unwanted bulbs and piles of our best topsoil waiting to be turned into camouflage around the gun emplacements. Once the guns were in place there followed the building of quarters for the crews. When we finally returned home after the war it was to the devastation of a lovely island turned into a gun-post.

✱✱✱

And then began the systematic inventory of every house, every building. Empty properties were requisitioned at once. Other properties in key areas were commandeered and families ordered to clear out and find a deserted property so that the military could move in. Empty greenhouses were used for the growing of vegetables.

When they came to Frederick's house, there was copious notetaking and discussion. A house with a bath and toilet was something different. For some reason they decided not to requisition it but to make use of the facilities. Several times a week officers would come and use the bathroom.

✳✳✳

And so began my relationship with the enemy. On certain days and at fixed times I would be told to make sure I'd been to the toilet and then stay away from the soldiers. A batman would arrive first to prepare the bathroom for the officers from the nearest gun-post and he would be on hand to clear up after them. They would queue up in an orderly way outside the house until it was their turn. There was always a lot of jolly chat between them but it was only when my mother complained and the routine was changed that I met them properly.

From the beginning although we had been ordered to be courteous to the Germans, local people defined this order in different ways. Most people wanted nothing to do with them. Some people, by nature of their jobs had to work with them, something easy to interpret as collaboration. A few of the girls were flattered by the attention of handsome young soldiers, something much deplored by the locals who saw this as a betrayal of the men fighting on the front line. And there were others too frightened to do anything other than comply with their requests. At the end of the war there were many false accusations of collaboration by people who had not fully appreciated everybody's situation. As one woman said, 'My children had been evacuated. I was on my own with a small holding and when at night the Germans knocked on my door demanding a chicken what was I to do? Whatever I had said or done it would have made no difference, they would have helped themselves.' So when a line-up of young officers was seen on a regular basis outside our house it was inevitable that those not close enough to know the truth saw it quite differently. My mother was upset. My father was deeply angry and determined to do something about it. But it was my mother who sorted it. Afraid of the consequences if my father confronted the authorities, she decided to see the German Kommandant herself. 'If he is any sort of gentleman,' she told my father, 'he will understand immediately what I am talking about.'

✼✼✼

Not only was he a gentleman he was also English speaking and faced with an indignant Ruth Cockayne he speedily came to an arrangement which suited both parties. There would be no more queues outside the house. Instead officers would be admitted to the conservatory where they would wait.

✼✼✼

At first there was a stand-off. Feeling the imposition of having her home invaded, my mother wanted nothing to do with them. They came. They left. The orderly always leaving last as he cleaned and tidied after the officers. When I came back from school I would join my mother in the kitchen and it was there that things began to change. One day one of the officers spoke to my mother. 'I wondered if you would allow me to give your little girl some schokolade?'

Chocolate. I hadn't understood everything he said with his German accent but I understood chocolate and looked eagerly at my mother. There was a long pause and then she said. 'It's very kind of you but...'

'Please,' the man smiled at me as if inviting me to be part of a conspiracy.

Suddenly my mother laughed. 'Oh, go on then.'

The ice was broken. From then on although my mother was always correct, there was a slackening of tension. Photographs were produced of girlfriends, wives, children and old parents. I supposed my mother realised that like the rest of us these young men were caught up in a war and missing their families. I don't ever remember our being frightened of them. When they could bring us something they did, chocolate, a little coffee. At that time they had better supplies than we did. And there was one day when I came home from school to find my mother sitting with her arms around a weeping young soldier. 'Margaret,' she said later, 'you are never to tell anybody about what you have just seen. We shall tell your father but no one else. That young man was crying because he is going to be sent to the Russian front where there is the most dreadful fighting. He would be in serious trouble if his commanding officer knew that he had told me about it or that he had not wanted to go.' She didn't add that he would have been taken out and shot. That kind of information I would only learn with the passing of time.

✳✳✳

School resumed, the teacher, a German, was tasked with teaching the children the German language and propaganda, preparing them for spot tests from the military. Health checks were done, height and weight recorded and a glass of milk allocated to every child with a substantial bean soup at lunchtime. Children soon learned not to repeat any conversations they heard at home and not to tell their parents that Hitler was a great leader.

To be occupied can only be understood by those who have experienced it. For Frederick Cockayne this was the end of everything he had worked for. The idea that he would stay and care for his vineries keeping everything safe and ready for the peace had been a pipedream. His land was requisitioned and his house was only spared because of the bathroom and the fact that as long as Frederick was there the complicated operation of the cess pit was in his hands. He was a man without a business. He was a man whose home was no more than a wash place for the army. Although he was no longer fit for active service he now regretted that he hadn't taken Ruth and Margaret to England which at one stage he could have done so easily. At least there he could have found war work, munitions, Home Guard, A.R.P. anything would have been better than this non-existence. He was a man and not a man. Four years in the trenches and for what, so that he could suffer defeat at the hands of his enemy? Each night as he watched the sky fill with search lights looking for "our planes" and knowing they could be shot down by the gun-post now occupying his land it was only his love for Ruth and Margaret that kept him going. For their sakes he must not take any chances, no crazy schemes to escape in a little boat, no listening to radio messages or trying to send information across the Channel. Fortunately he still had his faith and so long as his sermons were never accused of being inflammatory he was allowed to continue preaching but always with the presence of soldiers.

People were afraid. It was so easy to fall foul of the authorities. Newspapers were issued and posters hung from every wall or shopfront with a never-ending flow of regulations. There was never a day when you could be sure of what was going to happen. Add to that just trying to survive was challenge in itself. Laundries shut for lack of fuel and soap. The telephone was suspended. More and more foods were rationed. Shops closed, some for the duration, others with limited opening and long queues for what little they had to sell. At first only the civilians suffered but by the end of the war the army itself knew what it was to go hungry and to eat soup made from parsnip and cabbage leaves. Everyone was instructed to grow vegetables. Salt, which was rationed, was reclaimed by simmering seawater in a biscuit tin surrounded by a fire of sawdust. If you could get access to a bit of beach and find Carrageen Moss you would turn it into something which tasted sweet like blancmange. Cabbages were easy to grow and became the basis of every dish, slow cooked all night in a large bean jar. Potato peelings were found to have a lot of taste and bread might be made with horse's oats and sawdust. For those with money there was always the black market but as most people had lost everything they valued they were no longer in a position to take advantage of this even if they had been inclined to do so.

Children became scavengers. Because they were no longer allowed to play games in the street going out after school looking for food and fuel became a much more exciting pastime tinged with danger and enormous satisfaction when the enemy was duped. Some became remarkably adept at spotting unattended lorries or trucks being unloaded and they would play around waiting for the right moment to fill an old doll's pram with whatever they could pilfer. Most of the soldiers knew exactly what they were doing and chose to turn a blind eye and they learned to avoid one sergeant who threatened them with punishment if they kept on stealing.

A much more dangerous but highly successful game played mostly by adults was the collection and distribution of leaflets dropped by British planes and punishable by death. As civilian cars were no longer on the roads people used cycles but even those had their problems. Greenhouse hosepipe and rope were used to repair tyres while wooden soles replaced worn-out shoes and sandals. As far as the Germans were concerned the main thing was keeping the locals away from the roads, the transport of vital machinery sometimes by heavy horse drawn carts evidence that the island was being turned into a fortress.

It's difficult to imagine Guernsey in this situation, where people are starving and scared. Did the island become less beautiful to them during these days or were they still able to enjoy the glorious sunshine?

Despite their own misery and lack of food the islanders knew that there were some in their midst much worse off. The TODT organization with khaki uniform, red belts and Nazi crosses was in charge of the movement and control of slave labour, foreign nationals and prisoners of war whose job was construction for the military. 1600 slaves were sent to the Channel Islands to build massive fortifications, roads and railways without any thought for the land or even the homes of islanders. Soon, fury at the destruction of their homes and lands turned to pity for the poor creatures doomed to do this work. Treated like herded animals they were numbered and beaten and starved of food, fighting each other over snails on walls, eating both the flesh and the shells. Dressed in rags they worked day and night using cement bags to cover their bleeding feet and more bags to cover their heads and shoulders against the climate. The penalty for any contact with islanders was shooting.

❋❋❋

I was cycling home from school when I heard a strange noise behind me. Getting off my bike and pulling into the side I saw columns of men shuffling down the road, their clothes in rags, their bleeding feet inadequately wrapped in cement bags and leaving a trail of blood as they walked. I pushed my bike home as quickly as I could sorry but scared by what I had seen. I know my mother had seen them too and wanted to run out and give them some food but my father forbade it, much too risky both for her and anybody she helped. But I am sure my father gave them food at night when it was dark and he could pass something out without being seen. As for me, I couldn't talk about what I had seen. Were the Germans who marched beside these poor creatures, kicking and prodding them with their guns, the same Germans we let use our bathroom and bring us chocolates?

❋❋❋

And then, and as if what had already happened wasn't enough, there came a change in the Cockayne household that was to alter their lives forever.

Beyond the Wire

In June 1941 Persia, now known as Iran, was a neutral country whose largest trading partner was Germany. Taking advantage of this situation Germany sought to expand its already large ex-pat community with specialists in espionage and subversive activities, all of which compromised the neutrality of Persia whilst furthering the German war effort. Russians on one border and the British on another demanded that Persia expel all German citizens. Three times the request was denied and their agreement when it came was already too late as the Anglo Soviet forces, in a desperate effort to stop the seizing and sabotage of the railway system and precious oilfields, had invaded.

The German legation, women and children were allowed to return to Europe. Jewish Germans were permitted to stay but all Germans of fighting age, 18 to 45 were interned by the Russians in Siberia or sent by the British to India and Australia.

Hitler was furious and looked at once for reprisals, focussing his attentions on the Channel Isles, the only bit of British soil in his power. And despite being told by the German Foreign Office that British people there were effectively interned and could not leave without permission, he ordered the deportation of 10 Islanders for every German interned from Persia.

The two situations were completely different. The British Government was entitled to take whatever legitimate measures were necessary to stop the use of neutral territory as a cover for acts of war. Guernsey was an occupied country with the German military bound by the International Law of the Hague Convention which made no allowance for the internment or deportation of civilians already under military occupation so long as those people posed no threat to the military nor were they engaged in subversive activities. There was also Germany's ultimatum in the summer of 1940.

In the case of a peaceful surrender the lives, property and liberty of the peaceful inhabitants are solemnly guaranteed.

In 1941 the very threat to deport innocent civilians was enough to evoke loud condemnation from the British Government and when in 1942 that deportation became a harsh reality it was registered as a war crime and raised again in 1945 as part of the United Nations War Crime Charges.

German newspapers were full of the Russian atrocities against German civilians in Iran and of the reprisals Hitler was about to take. But although the orders had been given, when German women and children were returned to Germany via Turkey, the threat of reprisals stopped being the centre of everybody's fear and gradually people just forgot about it or the possibility of deportation.

The fact that it had been a direct order from the Fuhrer himself seems to have been either forgotten, (scarcely likely in the circumstances) put on the back burner or just possibly deliberately ignored. Product of the regular army the German Kommandant would have been well aware of the Hague Convention and the terms of the island's surrender. Added to which at the same time as the mention of the deportation he was instructed to take responsibility for the construction of fortifications on a scale so vast as to be unbelievable for an island measuring 27sq miles.

Was it that the Kommandant was more than happy not to have to carry out what he may have thought illegal and would certainly turn the locals against him. One thing was certain, he was unlikely to take it upon himself to remind the Fuhrer of what seemed like an oversight on his part. For whatever reason nothing was done and probably nothing would have ever been done had the matter not come to Hitler's attention again in the most unfortunate way.

Switzerland was neutral and in trying to effect the exchange of wounded soldiers for civilians, Hitler was reminded of the Channel Isles, his fury knowing no bounds when it emerged that nothing had been done. Now he reissued the orders himself but this time with lists and instructions. The requirement of 10 men born in the United Kingdom as reprisal for every German interned remained the same. And when his lists showed that there were not enough men who qualified he extended them to include women and children adding that properties and contents were to be confiscated and redistributed.

The lists and instructions were printed in the German Island paper.

From Guernsey

432 men aged between 18-45

359 men aged between 46-50

444 men aged 60 or over

1,525 women aged 18 or over

70 Children

Total 2,830

The Bailiff and other members of the island-based authorities refused the order from the Wehrmacht to deliver the official papers, demanding to know exactly what was in store for the deportees. Were they to be treated like hostages? Would they be deliberately billeted in towns directly in the path of Allied bombers? There were no answers, for the order came from the highest command, brooking no questions and giving no compromise. A demonstration against the order in Jersey resulted in arrests. In Guernsey there was a silent protest and soldiers were obliged to seek help from parish councillors regarding the whereabouts of the people who had been selected.

✳✳✳

I remember the evening. German military and Guernsey police came to the door with the papers urging my father to take heed and see that they must be completed and returned by noon on Friday of that same week to the Greffe office where the details would be collated and passed on to the Germans. An unnecessary exercise as this information was already to hand following on from the issue of identity cards with date and place of birth, service and rank in the armed forces and date of retirement.

Failure to comply would be punished by a military court. What I don't understand is why my father didn't put up more objection. He had been born in Belfast, a neutral country throughout the whole of WW2, but almost from birth his home had been Guernsey. He thought like a Guern, he worked like one, he married one, his child was one and never had a man loved his island more than my father. Exceptions were made for food producers, people in high positions and those in poor health. On the grounds of health alone both he with his single lung and my mother, who was chronically ill, could have been exempted. And after years as a successful grower surely he could have been put to better use growing food for army and civilians. For the rest, if you could walk you had to go, even women carrying small babies.

Was it that he still couldn't quite believe that he who had lived and loved his life on Guernsey should be challenged in this way? Was it that with the prospect of losing everything he had worked and strived for he was already a broken man? Or was it that he tried but that it suited the Wehrmacht for us to be removed? Our house stood alone now next to a gun-post and between it and other empty properties which the army had taken over and was already destined to be requisitioned.

❋❋❋

The evacuation had been bad enough, the deportation rocked the tiny island. Those whose names were not on the list were frightened and even more unsure of the future. If this could happen to people they had known and trusted all their lives what guarantees were there for anybody. The people on the list were in shock and at a time when they should have been thinking about what they needed to take and which arrangements to put in place were incapable of rational thought.

Chaotic scenes followed. Fear and panic prevailed. Some, unable to face the horrors of deportation, preferred to commit suicide. Many were convinced they were going to a concentration camp. Already they knew something of the atrocities committed in Hitler's endeavour to create a pure Aryan race. Quiet, law-abiding citizens giving no offense either to their neighbours or the occupying forces were being told to vacate their homes, surrender their goods and valuables and, taking only the bare necessities, leave their beloved island for an unknown, foreign and alien country.

✳✳✳

When we eventually returned home we felt the full extent of our loss both emotionally and financially. Property stolen or damaged beyond repair. Goods and valuables vanished. Loss of three years' earnings for which there was no compensation. Sickness, trauma and in many cases inability to hold down a job ever again, my father amongst them.

✳✳✳

Told to take only as much as they could each carry it was important that they choose wisely. The wealthy Cockaynes sported only finest quality leather suitcases substantially heavy even when empty.

✳✳✳

I thought it was not a problem for me. I had never had to carry a suitcase as we always had porters. And it was only when I was actually forced by a guard to take charge of my bag that I came face to face with the horrible truth. There were no porters and from the grim faces of the guards I realised that none of them was about to offer.

✳✳✳

The instructions had been clear. Warm clothes, heavy duty shoes and basic requirements in small suitcases together with a blanket to be carried individually with trunks packed with more clothing left ready to be shipped out later. It was a forlorn hope that they would be reunited with precious things to make their lives more comfortable. Only a few were ever delivered. Either they never arrived or the contents were stolen *en route*. Gradually people stopped expecting them.

***

Oh dear, a child always used to obeying chose this, the worst possible time, to rebel. My father told me to wear sensible shoes but he and my mother were so upset they never noticed that I was wearing my new most beautiful black patent leather with tiny straps. The joy of my life I was not about to be separated from them. Oh foolish child, not suitable footwear for an approaching harsh German winter.

***

A fund was opened to raise money for those in need. Cobblers worked through the night soling and heeling shoes and boots. Food was collected for the journey and one islander broke the curfew driving round the island in search of milk for the babies. And it was this same man who persuaded the Kommandant to let him cook a decent meal for them to have before they left. Field kitchens and German cooks were directed to assist him and between them they produced a hearty lamb stew. One can only conclude that not everybody in the German camp was in agreement with the Fuhrer's reprisal measures.

***

Not wanting to see friends and relations being marched from their homes the island committee, with the agreement of the Wehrmacht, laid on buses to collect us from our homes. I don't think anybody spoke during that last journey across the island. Everybody, even the children like myself, knew that something dreadful was about to happen. I think my father was trying to remember if he had told his brother Jack everything he needed to know regarding our property whilst we were away. Poor Dada, he didn't know that already the order to requisition our house had been given and that even had we been allowed to stay we would have lost our home and everything we possessed.

✳✳✳

The bus came to a halt outside the Gaumont Cinema from where people were marched to a requisitioned fruit export shed for documentation and medical examination. It was noticeable that after this was done, German soldiers and officials just sat around looking uncomfortable while islanders rushed about trying to do whatever they could to prepare people for the long journey ahead.

Extra-warm clothing and shoes were doled out to the needy. Wooden chip tomato baskets were filled with sandwiches, boiled eggs, precious chocolate, biscuits and even some English cigarettes.

When all was done, they were lined up and marched down to the jetty, passing pavements filled with people, some weeping, some openly condemning Hitler and the rest of Germany to everlasting damnation, whilst others called out messages of comfort and support. It was a procession watched in silence by German soldiers who made no response even when the marchers struck up with the national anthem and Rule Britannia. It says much for the sympathies of the German Kommandant who also chose to ignore this outburst from the local people.

Now though the attention of the deportees was directed towards the boats waiting to transport them across the choppy channel. A gasp went round as they took in the size and condition of two small ships. Obviously inadequate for the numbers travelling but more importantly not even seaworthy. The Germans were soldiers not sailors, with no knowledge of ships or the treacherous waters around the islands. The Guerns were a seafaring nation with hundreds of years of knowledge intrinsic to their nature and everyone, even the children, recognised a ship not fit for purpose. The men spoke first, strongly voicing their objections to their guards who merely shrugged and pushed them onwards urging their guns towards them until they were obliged to obey.

✳✳✳

My father refused to follow everybody going down the ladder into the hold and the already crowded wooden benches. Instead he found us a partially protected place on the deck where he wrapped us in our blankets before sitting down between us so that he could add warmth by enfolding us in his arms. I think I asked why we weren't going down into the hold like the rest. He answered somewhat distractedly that it was too hot and might make us sick. Many years later I learned the truth. My parents were worried that the conversation down in the hold would be about what we might expect in the future and deeply frightening for a small child. It was the filthiest boat I have ever seen and covered in coal dust, something we couldn't help but inhale and which impregnated our skin and clothes.

And then something wonderful happened, I heard voices calling out from the jetty. 'Margaret. Margaret!' Young officers who had shared our bathroom and been welcomed into our home. They came bearing chocolates and biscuits and something else too. Good news. They promised to move my mother's piano and the beautiful antique dining room furniture to a safe house. And they were as good as their word finding a van before the requisition order was carried out. It was a remarkable kindness and risky too defying a direct order from the Fuhrer.

***

The captain refused to put to sea and no amount of threats from the Kommandant would change his mind. 'Do you want to account for the death of the guards when the boat goes down?' asked the captain. When challenged that this was a gross exaggeration the captain raised two expressive hands and told him to find some other mug to sail it.

The boat did not sail that night.

***

It was a long cold night with the boat crashing against the jetty in the gale force winds and a steady stream of people coming on deck to use the only two primitive toilets the boat possessed. It was nearly dawn but still dark when exhausted and miserable we finally left. The deck was full of silent people as we sailed away from our dear rock. When the war ended not everybody would be going back and those that did bore the scars of their experience for ever more.

***

The Cockayne family had often visited St Malo, the nearest bit of France to the island but the St Malo they now saw was a different place. A garrison town and port it was seething with military and naval personnel. Security was at its height and the deportees struggling with their bags were hurried across the docks through the pouring rain and onto a train which would take hours to reach

Dorsten, a run-down prisoner of war camp known as Stalag VI in the heart of the industrial Ruhr valley.

***

It was a long journey in a dark unheated carriage with no more room than a cattle truck followed by a whole night in a siding in Cologne listening to the RAF bombing. A strange situation with people saying 'Give it to them' and cheering whilst actually being terrified that our own train was an ideal target. Just before we reached Dorsten we were all given a German sausage, bread and hot soup. I remember not being impressed by the sausage, an attitude I was to change quite soon when a sausage, even a German one, would have been devoured as a treat.

***

The women were taken by bus and the men by lorry to Dorsten where they were made to line up in the compound for counting prior to examination of papers and the handing over of all valuables. Medical examinations followed and mass vaccination. Some islanders, not realising the risks they were taking, didn't turn up believing they had been checked out adequately before leaving Guernsey. It was a hard lesson learning that from then on they had masters who would require immediate obedience or punishments would follow often with the withdrawal of food. They were to spend six horrendous weeks in this transit camp conscious that the barrage balloons filling the sky signified that they were in the centre of an allied bombing target.

***

I shall never forget Dorsten. Like the boat from Guernsey it was dirty, only this time with the filth that emanates from human beings living in terrible conditions. The previous occupants had just moved out and when we arrived it was obvious that the Germans were not ready. Apart from cleaning it up a bit it is hard to say what they could have done. The place needed rebuilding. Situated on a sandy plateau between a valley and below the level of a large shipping canal with lock gates badly damaged by an air raid it was close to local industry. As the weather deteriorated the fumes of sulphur increased, turning into a dense yellow fog from which there was no escape. Only the adults really understood the danger of our situation but even they had little time to dwell on this when they saw the primitive nature of our accommodation.

The German soldiers were housed in concrete buildings. My mother and I joined other women in disgusting old barracks while the men were given broken-down wooden huts which they tried to repair with bits of cardboard.

For me it was my first experience of sleeping in a dormitory with people who had different ideas about what constituted the makings of a good night's rest. Some wanted the windows open; others wanted everything shut tight. The huts were heated by slow combustion stoves and if you were tiny like me and pushed onto a top tier of three bunks you got more and more frazzled as the night went on. I don't think anybody pointed out that unlike the men we did have some form of heating. They had nothing. Looking back I realise the absurdity of quarrelling about open and shut windows when we had no idea what the future held or whether there would even be a future if the RAF made a direct hit.

Beds and fresh air were the least of their problems, the place was disgusting requiring deep cleaning. The toilets were insanitary and almost non-existent as they amounted to no more than slits in concrete over a hole and with no attempt at any sort of privacy. Even the islanders who were well used to outside privies had never experienced anything like this. After much complaining large, open cans were introduced. Marginally better.

There was little food and with nothing from the Red Cross at this stage, people's immune systems were constantly under attack so there was a steady stream of sick people wanting and needing attention from the few doctors and nurses who just happened to be amongst the deportees. There were three deaths including that of a baby during these first few weeks.

✱✱✱

And for me there was something else, something I just didn't understand, and that was internment. Used to being free to roam around at home, in the fields, down the lanes, by the sea, I would walk up to the great gates expecting to have them opened or pressing my face against the barbed wire, I would try to look out. The angry shouting in a language I didn't know and the presence of jackbooted soldiers with guns gesturing that I should move away frightened me and I would run crying to find my mother. Even as the years passed and as I became used to the camp and the fact that I couldn't leave I think I still found it difficult to understand why.

✱✱✱

Men were more used to taking orders and those who had been in the armed forces accepted this as a part of camp discipline, but women had no such experience, and took little notice of the Germans shouting for everybody to line up and be counted. Indeed they didn't think such instructions applied to them or their children so quite often when they should have been in an orderly line they were in other parts of the camp or playing with their children or simply gossiping in groups and no amount of shouting seemed to convey the urgency and the threat to their safety if they continued to provoke their guards. The roll-call could easily take an hour and as it was repeated three times a day it was both exhausting and tiresome.

Camp discipline was down to the Germans but its implementation and daily running were supposed to be the responsibility of the internees and quite quickly people began to sort out jobs and work out what was to be done to improve conditions. Food or lack of it was top priority so it was necessary to husband what they still had from the journey and that given to them by the Germans and apply strict rationing. Swede soup was issued twice daily with a little hard bread, jam or sausage and acorn coffee or mint tea. Nobody could eat the dried fish crawling with maggots and only desperation for food drove them to struggle with the boiled and unpeeled, muddy potatoes.

✳✳✳

And we were cold, so very cold. Called outside every few hours for roll-call, our extra warm clothes left behind in trunks supposedly for forwarding. A pleasure some of us were never to experience. I slept in my day clothes for a long time trying to get warm on a palliasse filled with wood shavings and covered with two thin blankets. Worst of all we were separated from my father. He was in one block and we were in another with a curfew at 10pm. For my mother this must have been so frightening. She wasn't well and depended on him for both physical and emotional support. For me it was like a terrible nightmare, something from which I kept expecting to wake up. They were my life, my all, my everything and even though they tried to make light of it I knew my mother's health was getting worse and there was nothing we could do about it.

✽✽✽

The death of the baby and the lack of milk for the children worried the Kommandant and paying for it with his own money he started buying milk from nearby prisoner of war camps and pressurizing for the delivery of Red Cross parcels all of which earned him the title of "Rosy Joe" from grateful mothers.

But the parcels were a long time coming because the German authorities had not informed the Red Cross or the British Government of the deportations. A two-kilogram loaf of bread had to feed six people on Sunday and eight people on other days. A daily personal ration of one and a half potatoes boiled in their skins every day. Riots broke out with people storming the kitchen and fighting each other. The first help came from the British officers in a local *Oflag* who on hearing of their plight sent what they could spare.

Eventually the longed for Red Cross parcels arrived.

Cigarettes
Plain chocolate
Tin of creamed rice
Slab of sugar
Packet of tea

Tin of condensed milk

Tin of hard dry biscuits

Tin of mixed boiled sweets

Tin of spam

Tin of jam

Tin of fatty bacon

Tin of salmon

Tin of butter or margarine, always rancid

It is easy to be deceived by a list. The reality was that with far too few Red Cross parcels everything had to be divided equally. Dividing and sharing were important jobs and only given to deportees who were thought to be honest and capable of taking a sausage and dividing it into eight perfect portions. Probably no more than a mouthful each but what a mouthful when you were so desperately hungry.

***

Dada was one of the chosen few.

***

There were one or two efforts at putting on concerts to cheer people and somebody tried to give the children some lessons but the conditions were so appalling nothing was going to succeed unless something could be done to improve the accommodation. Eventually a small committee approached the Kommandant with suggestions for work which the deportees would be willing to do themselves if they could have the materials.

Wanting to help but with no money or instructions to do so the Kommandant did the only thing in his power, he complained to the authorities that the camp was not fit for human habitation. Berlin sent an official to assess the situation. Was it the knowledge that already the Hague conventions had been broken by the deportation or the man's genuine concern about the conditions in the camp? Whatever the reason, soon after his visit the order came that there would be a mass evacuation to Biberach in Southern Germany.

It was about now and probably as a direct result of this visit that an Irish prisoner was repatriated to the Channel Isles on the grounds of ill health. The story he told the German controlled newspapers on the island was an amazing one of deportees helped all the way by smiling German guards who carried their luggage, of field kitchens set up on the train to provide food and of a beautiful warm camp all ready for their arrival, of food rations identical to those enjoyed by German civilians and of Red Cross parcels twice a month with more cigarettes and chocolate than had been available on the islands. A school had been started, dramatic and singing groups were highly popular while the football pitch adjoining the camp was in constant use and there had even been a trip to the local cinema.

It was a story that nobody believed any more than they believed the identity of the teller. Ireland remained neutral throughout the war so he would never have been in the camp in the first place. This was a massive propaganda stunt and either he was a German pretending to be Irish or he had been brain-washed into it. The question was why was this subterfuge necessary? Maybe it was because there were those in Berlin who thought the deportation broke the rules of the Hague Convention and should never have happened. If anything those back in the Channel Isles feared more for the welfare of their families and friends after this publication of blatant lies.

Dorsten to Biberach was another nightmare rail journey spent in the dark and, despite the arrival of winter, unheated carriages. No food, one drink in thirty-six hours and inadequate sanitary conditions compounded the misery as did the regular halts when soldiers, rifle butts at the ready, herded them off the train to stand in line to be checked.

***

The move, which we had hoped would be to a better camp, was not without worry. For all we knew we might be heading to a far worse fate. The real horror of the Holocaust had yet to be revealed but there had been rumours, many of them of concentration camps and unspeakable deeds. My parents didn't voice their fears in my hearing but I heard other people talking. So when we boarded a freezing cold train without food or enough water and with frequent brutal checks by the guards there were few people who didn't have grave concerns about their future.

Of course I wanted to know why we were in the dark most of the time. Looking back I see how hard it was for them to explain that we might be bombed by our own planes if we showed a train with lights. What child could possibly understand that kind of thinking? My father said something about there being a shortage of coal so why were other people so upset every time a plane went over? One woman toyed with her rosary the entire journey.

I was frightened as much by the dark as anything. It's important to remember that when we left Guernsey we left without toys or anything with which to occupy a small child.

My father took out the blankets again and wrapping me up, leaned me against him to sleep. But I was still restless so he and Mama took it in turns to tell me about the Rhine Valley which lay on our left and which had been one of their favourite holiday venues before the war.

It was a long time later that I realised what amazing people they were. Even in these terrible circumstances they could still find it in their hearts to talk about the beautiful Rhine Valley and relate its famous legends.

The train ran alongside the Rhine and when we left Koblenz we entered the valley properly and as my Mother told me, 'It's a curving river with rugged cliffs, large forests, hilltop castles and steep vineyards. All along are tiny villages with narrow cobbled streets and half-timbered houses decorated with window boxes of red geraniums and in spring the air smells of blossom and the whole region is full of strange and mysterious stories.' I sat up. If there was anything I liked it was a story. Well it wasn't going to be read, we had no books having had neither the time to choose favourites nor wanting to waste space in our tiny suitcases with heavy reading matter. It was a decision we were already deeply regretting. For the moment though I couldn't keep thinking about what was going on outside or the darkness or being hungry if a strange story was about to unfold and I shivered with expectation.

'There were two brothers and a blind sister,' she began, 'and when their father died he left money for the three of them, plenty for

everybody but the brothers were greedy and decided to cheat the blind sister.'

'And because she was blind she couldn't see what they were doing.' I interrupted, now really caught up in the story.

My Mother laughed, well pleased with my attention. 'Exactly. So when it came to dividing the gold pieces they gave the sister the same scoop as themselves but hers was turned upside down so that when she used it she would get only what could rest on the curved side of the scoop and was only a fraction of what they were getting. With their money the brothers built two castles or Schloss, Sterrenberg and Liebenstein. As for the sister with what little money she had she built a cloister at the foot of the two castles and before you ask, a cloister is a covered walkway in a monastery where the monks can walk and meditate.'

'So she was a good person?'

'Absolutely.'

'And the brothers?'

'Ah well their greed didn't bring them happiness. They quarrelled and eventually built a wall between themselves and when they'd wasted all the money they decided it was time to make friends again and to celebrate the reunion they planned to go hunting. The arrangement was that whoever woke up first would shoot an arrow at the other brother's window. Unfortunately, just as one brother was opening his window the other brother shot an arrow and it pierced his heart.'

I was speechless as my mother ended the story with the last brother going on his travels to the Holy Land to make his peace with God.

Emotionally exhausted I curled up closer to my father and slept for a while. But when I woke it was still dark and now I was clamouring for more tales of the Rhine.

It was my Father who took up the challenge while my mother dozed a little. 'The most famous story of all is the legend of the Lorelei. There once was a beautiful woman who was let down by her sweetheart and as was usual in those days if a woman didn't marry she might go into a nunnery to live a religious life away from people. Three knights accompanied her to the convent but on the way as they sailed down the Rhine she saw a steep rock and asked if she might climb it alone to see the view. At the top she thinks she sees her lost lover in the waters of the Rhine and in a desperate attempt to reach him flings herself from the rock to her death.'

'Do all the stories have a sad ending?' I asked.

'Oh the story isn't over quite yet. It is said that she lives on the rock combing her beautiful golden hair which distracts the sailors from their duties and they forget how dangerous are the waters of the Rhine, how heavy the currents at this point and crash their boats.'

I definitely went to sleep now but when I eventually woke I was eager for more stories and by now my mother, her head against my father's shoulder, had fallen into an exhausted sleep and it was left to my father to satisfy me. The tale he told was of a greedy little dwarf Alberich who stole gold from the Rhine and forged a magical ring. Wotan, the leader of the gods, needed money to pay his builders for a fortress and stole the ring, so Alberich put a curse on it. 'Everybody,' he said, 'who doesn't have the ring will want it and everybody that has it will be scared of losing it and will eventually be robbed of it and killed by its next owner.'

I think I must have fallen asleep at this point for when I next woke up Dada said we were nearly at the end of our journey. It was many years later when I was telling somebody about the journey and this strange story I was told that it was Norse mythology, and the beginning of the famous Der Ring des Nibelungen, part of Wagner's Ring Cycle.

❋❋❋

Biberach Camp, situated on a plateau 1800 feet above sea level and exposed to wind and weather lay in a bowl, surrounded by mountains and hills and had been chosen for its exposed position as a deterrent to ideas of escape. In any other situation you would have agreed that set in the Bavarian Alps and between the Danube and Lake Constance this was a truly beautiful old German town with its half-timber-framed houses and picturesque schloss.

The area had originally been set up as a showcase for German National Socialism and used as a Hitler Youth summer camp and with all the amenities you would expect. The difference being that in rooms designed to hold 18 the number was now more like 80. In Bergen-Belsen these rooms held 500. With the onset of war there was rejoicing in the town's local market square. Swastikas were flown and Hitler Youth occupied the front rows. The military took over the base but in no time it changed its role and became a prisoner of war camp with French soldiers being the first to occupy followed quite soon after by the much written about Oflag V-8. Twenty-six prisoners tunnelled 50 metres with the aid of spoons, knives, forks and empty tin cans, removing seventeen tons of soil in two months and although only four escaped and reached nearby Switzerland it was enough of a success for the whole unit to be removed to one much further from the border. Biberach then became what was called a transit camp for between two and three thousand Soviet prisoners but was in reality a place for continuing the systematic extermination of Jewish Bolsheviks with an expected death toll of seventy to eighty every week all shovelled into mass graves. This was no ordinary conflict where rules of war existed and Geneva Conventions respected. This was ideological, with clear aims in mind, part of which was the annihilation of Jewish Bolshevism. The Soviets were not considered worthy combatants but racially inferior. Political prisoners were shot on arrival.

It's a good thing that the true history of Lager Lindele was not revealed to the deportees until after the war. That they would have been forced to put up with it goes without saying but the knowledge of what happened there would have made life even more difficult especially for the women.

There followed a temporary camp for French and Serbian officers and as, according to the Geneva convention, imprisoned officers were not to be expected to do work and with few orderlies to perform any chores the upkeep of the camp soon fell into disrepair. At first the Wehrmacht had been only too pleased to hand it over to house the Guernsey civilian internees and the camp became known as Ilag V-B or Lager Lindele, Lindele Camp. Their pleasure was short-lived as they soon realised that, a crack regiment of the German Army, they were required to nursemaid old men, women and children. Far from making them more understanding of their prisoners, the knowledge seemed to fan the flames of their hostility and the word went round the deportees to be extra careful when dealing with the guards, not infuriating them further and certainly not making the mistake of being slow or unwilling to carry out orders.

***

It was snowing when we arrived. Stiff, tired, cold and hungry we stumbled off the train on to a station full of angry armed guards ready to use the butts of their rifles to push us into an orderly line before taking up their positions behind, in front and either side to march us to the camp. A mile away and with no offer of help not even for the old people but rather harsh words and more painful prods from ever ready rifles we began the painful ascent. Had we not been so tired and cold we might have noticed the charming old town with its half-timber-framed cottages.

***

What a motley crew. Women, children, babies, and men who were no longer in the first flush of youth all struggling up this agonisingly steep hill and carrying their few possessions in suitcases which had suddenly become almost too heavy to lift.

***

'You must help your Mother.' My father had taken care of their two bags and was leaving me to carry my own and support my mother who was in increasing distress. Poor Mama, so frail now but a tall woman, too tall for the kind of help I had to offer. Add to all this my

shoes, which following the destruction of my beautiful patent leather, my father had made by cutting down a pair of women's high heels which felt uneven, painful and awkward I was not only uncomfortable but deeply ashamed at not having taken notice of the order to wear warm sensible footwear. Eventually a Norwegian woman passed over a pair of her daughter's warm boots. But at that time there was no reprieve for the matter of the shoes and I don't think I have ever felt so unhappy, so alone and so guilty at being unable to help my mother who did so much for me. Now, when the roles were reversed, I was failing her. I felt the tears well up but swallowed hard trying not to let her or my father see. There were others who did and probably because they were much more frightened of any action the guards might take if the procession slowed down they removed the suitcases from my father allowing him to give full support to my mother, trying to keep her upright as she struggled through the slush and snow to Lager Lindele.

✳✳✳

At last they were there, and as the large gates closed behind them, they felt the full impact of the imprisoning barbed wire and the hostile unsmiling inspection of helmeted soldiers, training their guns from the tall watchtowers surrounding the camp. Some deportees had arrived earlier and had gathered together what food they could find to feed them. But there was to be no respite from the cold, fatigue and hunger. Instead, and despite freezing conditions, they were herded onto a large compound. 'Raus! Raus!' shouted the soldiers pushing them with their rifles into orderly lines ready for inspection and the checking of names against an official looking list. 'Eine. Swie. Drie.

Fere. Funf.' The count seemed never ending and the guards increasingly angry as the numbers and lists did not tally and they were forced to repeat the procedure again and again.

✳✳✳

I don't know how long we stood. I had never been so cold or so miserable. I think I went off into a kind of frozen trance, my body no longer able to function or register anything except the threatening behaviour of the guards. We had thought Dorsten was bad enough but here there was an enemy which openly hated us and against which nobody dared protest. I think by now our captors had made it abundantly clear what would happen if we didn't obey and we all stood, including my mother, now surreptitiously supported by my father and other people who took up places close by to add their strength to his. Eventually it was over and we were allowed to go to our barracks and finally have some soup and jacket potatoes. We were starving and fell on the food like a pack of ravenous wolves. It was one of the best meals I have ever tasted and even today when baked potatoes are served I can't help remembering that glorious moment.

✳✳✳

Because it had been used as a prisoner of war camp it was designed to control large numbers of escape eager men. There were twenty-three barracks surrounded by barbed wire with frequent observation posts.

✳✳✳

The Wehrmacht, objecting to the idea of looking after women and children, insisted that we be separated from the men and boys by a barbed wire fence and that we be allowed limited hours to be together, 10 to 11 in the morning and 3 to 5 in the afternoon. It was

114

long after the end of the war that I knew the truth about the camp's usage previous to our arrival and fully understood the Wehrmacht attitude. They were used to dealing with men and using whatever means they liked to keep order. How ignominious to be in charge of a group of old men, women and children. It was bad enough being deported but to be kept apart from my Father was the worst blow of all. He was the one who kept us going. He was the one who was strong enough to look after my Mother. He was the one who made us laugh. And as I looked at him on the other side of the wire and saw his anxious face I thought my heart would break. Now I did cry and Mother too although she was quick to point out that we would see him every day for a little while and we mustn't make him unhappy by telling him how miserable we were. That we were allowed to be with him a little time every day was no real consolation.

Before being allocated our barracks we were searched, medically examined, inoculated against typhus, photographed and our fingerprints taken. More evidence of the German obsession with facts and figures and not with any concern or interest in the people involved.

Mother and I were in B8 and Father was in 20. The barracks were largely single storey block-built buildings and a few wooden ones all housing eighty-four internees with as many as eighteen in a room in double-decker bunks. What I remember most, apart from always being hungry was the cold. We came from the mild climate of Guernsey where even in winter we had no need of heavy winter clothing. Winter in Upper Swabia was a different proposition. We were freezing, some of the men and boys still in the shorts in which *they had left home and the women with no thought of a need for stockings. And with little fuel for the stoves and the thinnest of blankets there seemed no way to get warm. Some local girls, hearing of our plight, threw pieces of coal over the barbed wire, much to the annoyance of the guards who shouted for them to go away, training their guns on them but with little intent on firing as the girls were pretty and enjoyed flirting.*

✳✳✳

People came and went from Biberach maintaining the excessive number of a thousand. Mostly they were Channel Islanders but at the end of 1944 the S.S. sent a hundred Jews from Bergen Belsen and in the following January a second group of three hundred from the same concentration camp. The internees had known their fair share of hardship and hunger but nothing to compare with what these poor souls had experienced. They bore obvious signs of the abuse they had endured, were half-starved, verminous, with rags for clothes. By this time the Islanders had little of their own left but they shared what they could and hunted out some clothes.

✳✳✳

This was my first experience of meeting and living with people of other nationalities apart from the German officers who came to our house. They looked and sounded different, some had quite dark skins others light olive, some spoke languages I had never heard before. Their clothing was falling to pieces and when you got near to them you could see they were filthy and smelled. My father took me to one side and I had my first and only lesson in what they now call race relations but which my father talked of as being the will of God. 'We are all God's children, every one of us including those poor unhappy souls you have just seen. How we look and how we sound does nothing to change that. So Margaret let us think what we can do to help.' And then he added something which I only understood many years later. 'Faith without works is dead.'

***

Crowded they were but that same amount of accommodation housed five hundred in the concentration camps so this was almost luxury. A central corridor separated its two halves with one side for the Barrack Leader and her Deputy. In the middle were the ablutions, and at one end a single abort, for ninety-two women. With the temperature at minus 15 they were all desperately in need of the contents of their trunks, something that people began to realise had just been part of the Germans wish to put a good light on the deportation.

***

By now after our experience in Dorsten we had accepted the lack of privacy although we never got used to it. We were all people sharing the same life-shattering experience so you would imagine that this would bring us together. Far from it. The differences between us seemed to be accentuated adding to our unhappiness and very probably to theirs. We have a tendency to cling to those like ourselves, who speak the same language and have the same values. To some my mother and I were snobs thinking ourselves a cut above the rest. To us some of them were crude, roughly spoken with every other word a swear word, something that never happened in our home for both my mother and my father were God fearing people

*who would never have taken the Lord's name in vain or indulged in
the colourful language of the work-place or drinking bars.*

✳✳✳

But slowly and as time passed there grew a kind of acceptance, a sort
of unconditional love which allowed for the differences and made
more of the likenesses, the kindness, the understanding, the generosity
and were about man's humanity to man.

✳✳✳

*Each person had their own bunk, a wood shaving mattress and thin
coarse grey blanket, a wooden stool and a small locker in which we
stored our few cherished possessions. In the centre of the room there
was a square wooden table and for heating a black cast-iron stove and
everybody was given a thick white china bowl and plate, an
aluminium mug and knife, fork and spoon.*

*For the first day or two we were all, even the children, too tired to
take in our surroundings properly. The stay in Dorsten had taken its
toll, the lack of food had robbed us of energy, the journey had been
exhausting and we all felt the real impact of being imprisoned. When
the order came for us to take showers I had no expectation of what
was to come. As usual we were lined up and marched to an area
between the inner and outer barbed wire fences. Later we discovered
that there were similar blocks to use as a school, a canteen, a washing
and drying room, a room for entertainments and leisure activities.*

*There were two hospital blocks and a camp police station which
was quickly called "Bow Street" with fourteen constables who were
responsible for seeing the barracks were locked at night and general
order. Not much of a job really as the internees were unlikely to do*

anything to offend their German masters in fear of being sent to a concentration camp. And then there was the "Big House" for German officers and the camp Kommandant's billet. It was here that we could feel the closeness of the lookout posts, with machine guns pointing in our direction and, at ground level, and close, soldiers patrolling with slavering, snarling Alsatian dogs. Their bark was enough to warn me they were not looking for a stroke.

We were herded into the showers and ordered to undress. I can remember standing there not understanding what had been said and wondering why everybody was looking at me to hurry up. The hut was full of women and children. I shrank closer to my mother. 'It's alright, Margaret.' I suppose she was trying to reassure me because when I think about it she and the other women must have felt exactly the same. And it wasn't alright for me, not at all. Brought up in a time when you were taught not to expose your bodies to anybody the idea of taking off my clothes in front of other people and standing there naked was not only embarrassing but felt a wicked thing to do. Added to which I had never seen a naked adult and daren't look at one now, indeed I was too scared to do so. I spent the entire time staring at my feet. But the warm water was comforting and as time passed I grew to look forward to the showers though I never got used to the naked bodies and always looked at the floor.

***

What followed was a period of uneasy calm. People stood around in groups not quite sure what to do next, the women waiting for the men to visit, the men anxious about the women and their children. All aware that the soldiers had little patience for their jobs as guards to a pathetic bunch of deportees, it was agreed that every effort must be made to minimise the friction between the two groups and the children must be told to stay within the boundaries of the camp and not try and venture further.

***

My father walked me round the perimeter of the compound pointing out the posts with unsmiling guards watching us all the time and ferocious looking dogs that leapt and snarled as they patrolled the barbed wire. 'They have a job to do,' he explained, 'and that is to keep us here.'

I think I asked, 'Are we prisoners, Dada?'

And he replied vaguely, 'Yes, for a little while, Margaret, we have to be patient.'

To a child a little while has no meaning. Five minutes is an eternity if you are waiting for something you want. A day is forever. The only reason that I didn't pester him every few minutes was that I was an obedient child and I knew he expected me to accept what he said and not make a fuss. They were the most loving of parents and their discipline was always gentle but firm. Looking back I think it was possibly this that helped me survive what for a child was an unnatural, cruel and frightening experience.

More recently I have tried to imagine what it was like for the adults in the camp at this early stage in the war, with Germany seemingly on the crest of a wave and years ahead of D-Day. The nearest hope they had was when the RAF carried out a bombing raid. A strange phenomenon of people cheering a raid which could have wiped them out in minutes.

***

Doctors and nurses took over the hospital block and the care of the large numbers of older people who were already suffering from malnutrition. A German surgeon was in charge assisted by a kindly hospital sister who supervised the two barracks, one for men the other for women. They, in turn, were assisted by internee doctors and St. John's Ambulance workers. Coarse rough sheets were provided, marginally better than the standard thin blankets issued for the rest of the camp. Babies were born and furnished with swastika stamped birth certificates, something which angered everybody. Most medical problems were sorted in camp but with only limited resources all serious cases, diphtheria, scarlet fever and meningitis were transferred to a large hospital in either Tubingen or Ulm. Even so it says much for the staff and the hygienic conditions in the hospital that despite the lack of drugs and medical equipment and even something as basic as hot water there were so few deaths.

***

But people did die and although the statistics show a remarkably low figure each one represents a personal and family tragedy and a terrible blow to the morale of the internees. Death in a foreign land behind barbed wire. What a way to go! Amongst the few at Biberach was my own dear Mother. It was in the Spring of that first year that our barracks became the camp hospital and Mama and I were moved out to B15. My mother was never a well woman and I suppose I was so used to this that when she became sick I don't think I treated it as other than the norm. By now we had become so used to the lack of comforts. No cosy blankets, no hot lemon and honey, no opportunity for the loving care of a devoted husband. Hardened to our surroundings we observed people feeling unwell with a certain acceptance. It was what one expected in harsh conditions, with poor food and little hope. Today we talk about immune systems and mental health both of which must have played a big part in my mother's decline. All her life she had enjoyed a protected life among quietly spoken, gentle people and suddenly she was transported to share primitive conditions with loud-mouthed women used to standing their corner. The men in their barracks overcame some of these differences with a humorous camaraderie that covered all sorts and conditions of men. When everyone is struggling to survive there is little time or emotion to spare for the weaker amongst us. Even I noticed without really realising how poorly she was. After all what could any of us do? I think one or two of the women tried to make a hot drink for her but mostly she just lay in her bunk waiting for the hour when my father would arrive. It was soon clear to him and the internee doctor that she was seriously ill and she was moved out of the barracks and into the hospital area. It was now that I began to worry. Mama had always been there for me and suddenly she had gone away and without my father to turn to I became more and more isolated, despite the endeavours of some of the women to comfort me.

As each day passed my need for her grew and now, almost angrily, I demanded to know where she was, desperate to see her, to be in her arms, hear her reassuring voice. Eventually Dada got permission to take me into the ward. I can see her now as she lay so still, her rich brown hair sprayed around her pillow. 'Mama,' I cried, my heart breaking with joy and if Dada hadn't been holding my hand I would have run towards her, climbed on the bed and buried my head in her shoulder. But even as I pulled forward she turned her face to the wall and my father, grasping my shoulders wheeled me outside. I don't know what explanation he gave at the time but I did not hear it. I could hear nothing and feel nothing except the pain in my heart. My mother hadn't wanted me. When I so needed her she had turned away. She did not love me, had probably never loved me.

Years were to pass before I fully understood what had happened and that it was her deep love of me that made her turn in her grief to the wall. Dada had understood but how does a grieving man explain this when his own heart is breaking? How do you tell a small child living in dreadful conditions and so far away from home that, to add to it all, her mother is dying and that she turned to the wall to try to protect her daughter from seeing the extent of her own grief as she faced the knowledge that all her loving plans, the wonderful future that she had planned to share with her dear little daughter would come to nothing. Perhaps Dada said something about her needing to rest until she gets well. Lies. Lies. Lies. Looking back I wonder if it wouldn't have been better if I had been allowed to face up to the dreadful truth that day and seen my mother weeping and shared her tears. Later I could have mourned her loss, wept more tears and kept a place in my heart for her forever. Adults do what they do, make decisions they think are for the best, try to spare the young grief without taking into account the lasting damage that may result.

For me the damage had been done and for years there was a stone in the place where my heart had been and I could not visit Mama's grave with the love she so rightly deserved. It was meningitis and Mama was transferred to a large civilian hospital.

I was placed in the care of two women while, so they told me, Mama was made better. They were both kind and did their best to help me but soon, because I suppose everybody knew my mother would not get well again, I was asked to choose one to live with. What a choice for a small girl. I knew neither of them properly. One I had never seen until now. The other I recognised as somebody who was always rushing about the camp. But I had actually heard her laugh, something so rare that when it happened everybody stopped to listen. That decided it. She was a leader in one of the barracks and cared for the women with young children. But there would be no reprieve from that deadly disease and it was only a matter of days before Dada came to tell me, 'My loved one is buried in a beautiful garden.' I remember some of us hugged him and then we just got on with our lives, the business of one day following another, the survival for existence. For me her death had already happened in the camp hospital the day she turned her head away. I was angry and felt let down that she had allowed herself to die when even if she didn't love me she had a duty to share the burden of the camp with everyone else. It was an anger and bitterness that was to stay with me for years, a grief so deep that whenever it came into my mind I had to push it away and focus on something else. I could scarcely talk to my father who was still mourning long after the war was over and indeed until he died, not just for his loss but full of self-blame for his part in the matter of their deportation.

Channel Islanders were afforded proper burial and records kept but for the Jews who joined them there was no such respect. Indeed they were carted away with no deference to their passing or the nature of their burial.

***

In my search for the truth and to gain more insight into the nature of my father it is necessary to look at all aspects of camp life but for me all these years on it is this part, the loss of my mother that is hardest. And inevitably the question, the same, same question. Why did my father let it happen? He had the money. He had the means to whisk us away. So why not? And he loved her to distraction. She was the sun, the moon and the stars for him. Everything he did was for her. So why, oh why, did he not protect her from this?

The fact that babies were born suggests that despite the limited number of hours together and in spite of crowded conditions men and women still found opportunities to make love. That a child might be a natural outcome did not seem to deter them nor more importantly that they were creating another mouth to feed when there was so little food for everybody else. I have a vague recollection of my mother speaking of giving people quiet time together or not going near certain bunks when couples were supposedly sleeping. If the weather was good then she and my father would urge me out of doors to walk around the perimeter or play with a mangy old ball that the prisoners of war had left behind. I can't imagine what my parents must have actually thought, they were so restrained, so undemonstrative and sex so private, or was it that in the present situation they accepted people as they were and their basic needs too.

Presumably the segregation of the sexes, especially at night was to prevent just this happening. The last thing the Germans wanted was a camp full of squawking babies requiring more attention and extra milk. Did they do anything to stop it?

***

The internees were expected to be responsible for the general running of the camp and leaders were chosen to monitor behaviour and draw up rotas for the essential jobs like cleaning and fair distribution of Red Cross parcels. The sending and receiving of post was of considerable importance to both the Islanders and the Germans, both searching in vain for hidden messages about the war. Families were allowed to receive censored postcards of twenty-five words via the Red Cross and German *Feldpost*. The reality was different as the infraction of camp rules or loss and misplacement due to progress of war meant that post, when it was received, was infrequent and out of date. The last thing anybody wanted was to involve Germans in petty squabbles which might result in more camp regulations, so the setting up of a camp police manned by internees was agreeable to everyone. A Camp Marshal and fourteen constables were elected to maintain discipline, check security, deal with procedure during air raids and generally oversee camp behaviour. The most difficult job was that of Camp Captain, the overall leader of the internees who had the painful task of negotiating with the German authorities on behalf of the internees and also ensuring that German regulations be respected and obeyed. It was a job that won him few friends in either camp but he was widely praised by the International Red Cross who found him a strict but just leader and praised him for his continued efforts to raise standards and improve spirits. The day-to-day running of the camp was a huge job in itself and he was always trying to find ways of improving conditions and bringing some pleasure into the lives of these unhappy people. They were often simple things but the amount of effort that went into their execution could take hours of skilful negotiating. One year he secured three Christmas trees, another a barrel of beer. Few people really understood how hard he worked, often with little or no return. Of particular importance was the behaviour of the children who must on no account be a nuisance, especially to Germans on duty. This was one of the more difficult assignments as small children move quickly and have a habit of getting into the wrong place at the wrong time and there were quite a few occasions when a small child had to be scooped up pretty smartly as they strayed into forbidden territory. Everybody was supposed to salute officers, something the internees found particularly unpleasant.

***

I actually remember one or two of the soldiers laughing and giving me a wave as I was carted away. I suppose that some of them were fathers and knew exactly how young children behaved and maybe thought some of the restrictions unnecessary.

***

With such a diverse group, camp discipline was essential and although everybody hated the three daily roll-calls at 8.45am, 11.00am and 5.45pm they did act as a means of binding the group into some sort of orderly assembly. They also unified the camp for a short time against the enemy instead of against each other. The trouble was that instead of them being speedily carried out they seemed never-ending as the

Germans miscounted and recalled the internees again and again despite the freezing weather. The general consensus of opinion was that the Germans couldn't count and what kind of a system was it anyway? What the deportees didn't know was that many German games involved the figure five, Doko, Rein Stick, and 5 Crown Rummy. It was thought by German High Command that even an uneducated German soldier would have no problem counting up to five. In that it would seem they were wrong, for the mistakes in the counting and then the process of adding on the count were too difficult for many of the lower ranks.

Routine was necessary and as far as the Germans were concerned normal practice with or without a war. They were and still are a law-abiding nation enjoying a fascination for figures, records, inventories and statistics. The meticulous recording of names, numbers and unspeakable atrocities within the concentration camps was less about the crimes committed and everything to do with the German obsession with record keeping. To many of the deportees it was just one more thing to add to their misery and totally unnecessary in a camp largely full of women, children and older men who had no intention of trying to escape, indeed had nowhere to go. The day was divided up into segments, roll-calls, once a fortnight showers, visiting times when the men and boys could join the women and of course meals which, despite the meagre offerings, had to be consumed at regular times in order to see that everybody got their fair share.

Committees were set up to organise interests which would focus people's attention on something other than their plight and because the previous occupants, all energetic young officers, had made use of the extra barracks for entertainments and education it made sense for the internees to do the same. Everybody was invited to share their expertise for the benefit of the camp.

A drama group was started and with a fairly mixed bag of musicians an orchestra began to practise. If you were passionate about either of these activities never again would you be able to devote to them so much time. Concerts and dances were planned and even non-dancers were encouraged to move around for the exercise, an activity that would gradually lessen as food grew scarcer and bodies weaker, but even then they liked the music and swayed in time and sang along with it. Once a ball had been provided the men and boys devised all sorts of team games and when the weather was better there were always people out in the compound. When the women began Keep Fit classes a wave of enthusiasm spread around the camp and it wasn't just from the participants. With noses pressed close against the barbed wire plenty of men turned out to witness the daily entertainment. It was a purely seasonal pursuit as the onset of winter meant that for many months, with a temperature dropping to between -15 and -20, there were few who left the protection of their barracks except for the agonisingly cold thrice daily roll-call. And of course there were lots of small classes pursuing all manner of interests from dressmaking or repairing the now threadbare clothes to designing boats whilst wishfully thinking of a return to Guernsey.

But there was another side to the camp, one which rarely features when we are talking about the effort people made to survive the years and the conditions. There were those who could neither sing, act nor play and what is worse had no wish to take part in any activity be it leisure or linked to the smooth running of the camp. A visit from the Red Cross noted their concern about the attitude of some of the internees, the prevalent depression, and listless apathy to any form of work. And with nothing to interest them friction and squabbles increased over the distribution of food and equally often over petty matters that rarely rated the time spent on their resolution. The idea that sharing a problem would bring people together never happened, if anything they became so self-absorbed that they were incapable of looking beyond their own needs, out of which grew greed and selfishness. Indeed as time passed the quarrels grew worse and eventually, with the agreement of the Red Cross and in a desperate attempt to maintain order, there were occasions when the Captain removed access to food parcels until camp discipline had been restored.

***

For me this was the beginning of a completely new life and one which would affect me for the rest of mine. Up to that point entertainment as such never featured in the Cockayne household. But when my mother died and I chose to be cared for by Mrs Olive Medwell things were about to change. Known to the internees as Nursey and to me as Auntie Ol she was a thirty-year old Deputy Matron married to Ted who became Uncle Ted and who had been Deputy Master of Guernsey's Town Hospital which served as workhouse and institution for the geriatric population.

They were as unlike my parents as it was possible to be. They partied. They drank. And as for Auntie Ol, she smoked, wore trousers, make-up and unforgivably she swore for which I had always believed

God would strike you down. Well he never struck Auntie Ol. She was one of the happiest people there and she never looked as if she feared the wrath of the Almighty. Used to a full social life she and Ted were not about to go into isolation especially in an internment camp and they were at the forefront of any activity especially if it signified having a good time.

Looking back I wonder what my life would have been like if Mama had lived. I can't imagine that she or my father would have allowed me to do most of the things to which Auntie Ol introduced me. Was I too young in those days to complain or question adult decisions and would my parents have overcome some of their problems in the camp and allowed me to join in because they wanted me to be as happy as possible in the circumstances? I loved my father dearly but even he was remote, imprisoned as he was for much of the day in his own barracks. By the end of the war I was sufficiently brainwashed by Auntie Ol to expect a different life from the one I had enjoyed before the deportation. And as the years passed I danced, I partied, I went to concerts and the theatre and yes I drank but there was one thing I did not take up. Swearing. Not for any religious reason but because it has always struck me as an unnecessary violation of a perfectly adequate language.

I was sent to share a four-bunked room with Auntie Ol and her deputy Auntie Irene. I had the top bunk and they had the lower ones. They were so kind and fun in a way I had never known so that although I missed being with my father and because I was confused over my mother's death I was as happy as it was possible to be.

Keeping warm was a major problem. Our blankets were too thin and our clothes more suited to Guernsey summer than a German winter. We came from an island where the coldest even in winter was never lower than 6.5 degrees and here where it was currently -15. Our only form of heating and indeed of cooking was a stove which burned briquettes made from coal and sawdust. Everybody was on the scrounge for anything that could be used as fuel.

It was a bitterly cold night and Auntie Ol had looked everywhere to find something extra to burn when she had an idea. I caught her looking at me with a keen eye almost as if she was measuring me up. 'Why didn't I think of it before?' she smiled at me. 'You're small, in fact you're tiny.' She couldn't have been more right. I was small when we left Guernsey. Now like everybody else I seemed to have shrunk. 'All that wood to spare.' Within seconds she had removed the bottom plank of my bunk-bed and in no time part of it was burning merrily. It was an idea that was to catch on, with the shortest of us being systematically robbed of our beds. Great care was taken to redistribute the remaining planks and all was well until the night when the gap between the planks and the mattress grew too great and I fell through, landing on a sleeping Auntie Ol who fought and punched and pummelled her unexpected assailant until, like an avenging angel, she rose from her bed, seized me in her powerful arms and shaking me like a rag doll restored me to the bunk, which Auntie Irene had repositioned, with a stern warning not to fidget. But the episode had not gone unnoticed and Auntie Ol was in some trouble with the authorities for destruction of property. Not that my bed was ever replaced and I lay curled up in a tiny heap avoiding the gaps and Auntie Ol's anger.

And that was not my only contribution. We were all responsible for the care of the cutlery and crockery that had been issued on our arrival. Everything had to be accounted for and if anything was broken there was no easy way to get replacements. The pieces had to be collected in their entirety and taken to the storeroom where a certain Christian Gerster would replace the broken item but not before interrogating the owner with a string of loud obscenities. Deportees responded angrily. Would he be kinder to a child, Auntie Ol wondered, especially a little one? It could only be me. The sacrificial lamb. They were visits I grew to dread, standing with my hands neatly folded while he shouted and roared. Did he really believe that one child was capable of breaking so much pottery and was the shouting all about the ridiculous deception?

Every morning male volunteers arrived with a large can of mint tea which was ladled out into our mugs. At least it was hot. Sometimes we had ersatz coffee made from acorns. The still hot grains were used by any woman lucky enough to have a water bottle as a means of warming their cold beds. Once cooled the acorns became tobacco for the men. Lunch was the biggest meal of the day. We might have soup. I remember the swede especially. It was thin and watery with pieces of fat and maggots crawling over it. On other days we would have one and a half potatoes boiled in their dirty skins and a fifth of a loaf of black bread usually a month old and covered in mould. Cheese and sausage doled out in minute portions had to be divided into even smaller equal amounts so that everybody had the *same. You have to understand that if you are genuinely hungry you will eat anything and neither criticise nor ask questions. As a child I did what was expected in those days. I was seen and not heard. Even so I sensed the fear, the anxiety that what little we had we might lose so easily.*

***

A committee was formed to deal with the arrival of Red Cross parcels. Although desperately needed they were also the cause of quarrelling and fighting. When you are hungry, really hungry, you will do almost anything for food and so it was with the internees, civilised people normally, who became something else in the struggle to survive. Even the committee set up to see fair rationing of every single item was suspect. A sausage divided into eight portions would be scrutinised to see if every portion was identical to every other and those who did the dividing were subjected to both physical and verbal abuse. Some things were shared out by allowing everyone to come to the centre and choose one piece for themselves. Every piece of food, even tins, were stabbed right through with a sharp tool so they could not be hoarded and used in an escape. The idea that anybody at Biberach would escape or even plan one was ludicrous. It was a camp full of middle-aged, elderly and old men and women and children all incapable of carrying out any bid for freedom. Their main aim in life was to survive the war which, even in the worst of times they believed the Allies would win, and return to Guernsey.

The children were sent to school in one of the huts and there followed several years of inadequate education that was to make life difficult after the war. The few teachers amongst the internees drew

up a timetable and other people with no qualifications were drafted in
to talk about their field of expertise.

✳✳✳

*At first we had no books and no writing materials but then somebody
found the stubs of old pencils and a wad of used bridge scoring cards
left behind by the previous occupants. You cannot imagine our delight
at having the means to write, but immediately their use was rationed.
We had to be careful not to press down hard, the pencils had to last,
the card had to be used over and over again and just how long would
one small rubber go on erasing? Eventually the Red Cross sent us one
or two books, some writing materials and playing cards, draughts, and
chess. There was universal rejoicing amongst children and adults. I
remember my father walking about all day with a smile on his face. If
there was one thing he had always enjoyed it was a game of chess. In
no time he had helped organise a chess tournament while around the
camp people were meeting to play whist and bridge and the children
were loving the feel of a full length pencil and reading a story from
one of the few books that arrived, for though the Red Cross wanted to
help us with our leisure hours, their first priority, indeed ours too, was
food of which we had barely enough.*

*There were mixed feelings when a request was put in for musical
instruments but when they actually arrived people realised what a
difference music might make to their lives and disapproval swiftly
vanished. Concerts and dances were organised, but as time passed the
dances also became concerts when we listened to well-known tunes,
no one having the energy to dance anymore. Sometimes a couple
would get up and sway to the music and other people would sing and*

tap to the sound. A drama group was established and when the Red Cross sent a copy of a play there were no end of volunteers wanting to take part or form the stage crew to create costumes, lighting and scenery.

✳✳✳

Religion played an important part for some people in their struggle to cope with camp life. Ministers of both Church of England and Methodist persuasions had been deported and set up regular hours for service and prayer. Their appeal for a means of heating a room was refused on the grounds that Germans worship in unheated churches, why shouldn't they? The Catholics had no resident priest but an old German Father offered to visit the camp once a week to say Mass, a visit eagerly anticipated by children of all faiths as the Holy Father was known to carry sweets in the deep pockets of his coat.

Soon after their arrival it was Christmas. Whilst acknowledging that Jesus was the son of God the Cockaynes had never celebrated Christmas believing it to be a man-made festivity with no credence from the Bible. So when people started talking about trying to make something of it they were not only less than enthusiastic they had absolutely no idea of what was involved. Peace, simplicity in all things, equality of their believers and obedience to Christ were the hallmarks of their religion but believing that faith without works is dead they knew that something else was needed to help raise the internees' low morale. So letting others take the lead, but now regarding it as a charitable act, they joined in the Christmas preparation to see if they could help provide something to cheer the children. With no materials they were dependent on what people could spare from their few possessions. The women made and dressed dolls. They scooped sawdust out of the mattresses to fill bodies made with the aid of a man's shirt, while Ruth Cockayne gave a pair of pink crepe de chine cami-knickers for the faces and somebody donated a brown woollen jumper to unravel and use for hair.

✳✳✳

I can scarcely believe that my mother would have taken such delicate lingerie with her or was it that it all happened too quickly to pack what she really needed or that deep down she just couldn't begin to visualise the harsh realities that faced them.

Whilst everybody complained at being away from home at Christmas, I was having the first Christmas of my life. People sent each other cards made out of all sorts, mostly food packets and matchbox covers and they strung them up around the barracks using bits of string from the Red Cross parcels. At home if anybody sent us a card it was always placed face down so that we couldn't see it. The idea of filling a stocking with all sorts of novelties would have been considered frivolous almost verging on the sinful. People were singing carols and laughing a lot as if it was all such fun. I'd heard them at school but we didn't sing them at home. We sang hymns to my mother's accompaniment or listened to the radio. Those who had instruments played Christmas music. We were served with potatoes and gravy for lunch and pudding from a Red Cross parcel for tea. I couldn't have been happier. Indeed the whole of that Christmas week we enjoyed an amazing menu. Swede, cabbage and barley soups were followed by potatoes in jackets, dried fish, and one day for a treat we were given the strange but immensely satisfying sauerkraut and gravy with mashed potatoes. It was years after the war before I could face soups in any form.

But the highlight of my Christmas was a present, an actual Christmas present in the shape of a doll whom I instantly called Carole copying other girls who seemed to think it an appropriate name for a doll at that time of year. She went everywhere with me, sleeping beside me in my narrow lumpy bunk-bed, walking round the compound and being held up for the guards to count although there seemed to be an opinion that as they couldn't count up to five adding another body albeit a doll would have confused them further. Carole was the first of two presents and arrived when my mother was still alive. The second came later at the instigation of Auntie Ol. 'That child,' she referred to my dear Carole, 'that child needs a pram. All babies need prams, Margaret.' I was agog. A pram! 'Leave it to me and Uncle Ted.'

When you have nothing everything that arrives has a value even if only for trading, so everybody had a use for the empty Red Cross boxes that had held our tinned food and it was with great difficulty that Auntie Ol persuaded the keeper of the boxes to part with two for me. The Captain, the keeper of the rough string which bound the parcels, measured out a length and, armed with a knife and fork for cutting and making holes, Auntie Ol and Uncle Ted put together a doll's pram to which a kindly member of the repair group added a bit of old woollen jumper to act as a blanket. It was a great occasion when I first put Carole into her pram and covered her up ready to go to sleep. Next to Carole it was the most important thing in my life. A pram with a square hood, no wheels and dragged about by a piece of *rough string. I don't think I had ever been so happy as I wandered around the compound talking or singing her to sleep. Today, when I see little girls pushing their expensive prams with their talking, moving, peeing dolls, I wonder if their joy can ever be compared to mine that day long ago in Biberack.*

***

As time passed the Wehrmacht handed over the running of the camp to the Home Office. As far as they were concerned it was an imposition and total waste of their trained manpower to spend time controlling women and children, and men too old to be of fighting consequence. Frustration showed itself in their rough handling, both physical and verbal, of the internees, their total disregard for age or frailty or for the freezing conditions into which they were subjected.

So, the change-over couldn't come too soon with the internees welcoming moving away from military to armed police with, hopefully, a more relaxed approach. What hadn't been expected was that the inadequate food they had endured would become even less with the introduction of civil law. German civilians were also feeling the pinch and were unlikely to give their rations to feed enemy internees. But the attitude of their new guards was indeed a welcome change. Quite a few were middle-aged Germans who had fought during the First World War and immediately identified with some of the men.

***

My father was such a one. I would often see him chatting in a mixture of English and broken German to one of the guards about their shared wartime experiences. It was a move unlikely to win him friends amongst the many in the camp who regarded all their guards, good, bad or indifferent as part of the same Nazi party with Hitler at the helm. My father saw people differently, recognising that most of us get caught up in wars that we don't want, sometimes don't fully understand, and so we have much in common with our so-called enemy.

✳✳✳

And there were others amongst the guards, poor miserable crippled men who had fought on the Russian Front and been invalided out to make what they could of their future lives.

✳✳✳

When I saw them I remembered the young soldier who had wept in my mother's arms at the news that he was to leave for the Russian Front. Had he died from starvation and lack of proper clothes and shoes in the freezing conditions, or had he been shot in hand-to-hand fighting or been mowed down or blown up by tanks or air bombardment?

✳✳✳

With the arrival of the civil guards things began to change. Instead of a military Hauptmann the camp came under the control of a Deputy Kommandant and Senior Guard Herr Otto Liebe. Liebe tried to do his best for the prisoners although handicapped by official rules and regulations and with an ever increasing shortage of food and fuel. With him at the helm Red Cross parcels were handed over to the committee in their entirety, making it easier for the fair distribution of food. Now too the restrictions regarding the separation of men and women were relaxed a little, so that families could get together, pool their resources and eat as a group. The men would bring over their potato ration and anything else they could find and perhaps, using a tin of Red Cross salmon, the women would make fishcakes and cook them as best they could on the stove with its briquette plank fuel.

***

Put like this it doesn't sound too bad. The reality was something else. A small tin of salmon, a potato and so many people sharing a couple of fishcakes. They were such a treat but I was always left so hungry, so desperate for more.

***

Eventually the internees were allowed out of the camp. A strange thing considering the increased bombing by the RAF. The walks were controlled, groups of about 100 people with armed guards front and back. But while some rejoiced at the prospect of a little freedom from the camp, there were many who were now too weak, too old or infirm to take advantage of the opportunity. Add to this growing number the children who were either too young to take part in the walks or hadn't the energy.

***

I can't begin to tell you what this meant to us all. Years of confinement in barracks and compound. And now thanks to a new easing of rules we were allowed outside, not to mix with the locals or go into the town proper but for a walk in the woods where we could collect pine cones, twigs and branches. Sometimes we went to what I used to call the Scary Wood. Douglas Firs standing so tall that they shut out the sun and if there was a mist it was really eerie. I used to hold on to Auntie Ol's hand and she would try to distract me and get me busy looking for the pendulous cones to take back to the camp. The guards didn't seem to mind our bending down to pick up wood for our stoves. *My father would collect a good bundle for Auntie Ol and I would make my own contribution of sweet smelling pinecones which scented our barrack room. I so loved those walks, especially when we saw wild flowers and if the guard let me I would pick some. There were bright yellow celandine, wood anemones, marsh marigolds, bird's eye speedwell and of course toadstools that some people called mushrooms and had to be discouraged from bringing back to eat. After the walk I would be starving and longing for something more than thin soup or a tiny portion of sausage. Even so those were special days and only happened if the Kommandant was in a good mood.*

✳✳✳

It was about this time that the Kommandant came up with an idea which caused considerable trouble in the camp. Farm and landowners were desperately short of manual labour. All the young men were at the front and many of the older men too, the rest were busy making munitions. An inadequate labour force of the old was left to tend gardens and farms. The Kommandant suggested that some of the men might like to work in the fields and gardens, without pay of course, and under the supervision of the families concerned who would take responsibility for collecting the internees and returning them to camp later that day. It was much the same thing that was happening in England. Farms run by a hard-pressed Land Army were in need of help. German prisoners of war with no known affiliation to the Nazi party or the SS and demonstrating good behaviour were drafted in to supply labour, being deposited and collected by armed guard each day. It was a scheme unlikely to meet with public approval. The idea of German soldiers who had fought and killed being given the freedom to move about was not to be borne and people would stand and stare, some in silence, others shouting verbal abuse as the soldiers passed by. So it was scarcely surprising that in Biberach internees deported illegally from their homes, deprived and starving, and hounded by the enemy at every turn would dig their heels in and refuse to do anything to help them grow food or anything else for their captors.

✻✻✻

There were a few who did not immediately react against the idea. Deep down they shared exactly the same feelings as everybody else. Why should they help a nation responsible for removing them from their homes to the hardship of captivity? My father had more reason than most to hate. Hadn't he lost his love, his life, his all when my mother died? They loved and were still in love when the combination of mental and physical torment and a depleted immune system drove her to an early grave with the onset of meningitis. So you have to understand the nature of my father to even begin to follow his strange reaction. Heartbroken with the loss of Ruth and probably because of his religion, apart from reading what few books were available and playing chess, he had few shared interests, no hobbies and no clubs which he would have wanted to join. He was a desperately lonely man with a small daughter separated from him for most of the day by barbed wire. So the idea of doing physical labour in the fresh air away from camp squabbles was deeply attractive. Added to that was a long-

held belief that anything which bound people together rather than separated them could only be for the greater good. It was progressive and at that stage in the war wishful thinking on his part and many years ahead of what nations might eventually recognise as the way forward. He was also mindful of the kindnesses shown to us as a family by young German officers both at our bungalow and in those last moments on the quay. If the roles had been reversed he knew how grateful he would have been for any help. And there was always the possibility that once outside the camp there might be opportunities to bring back something to help our miserable lives. He volunteered to work on the land. It was inevitable that politically minded patriots sought to make much of his decision. Traitor and collaborator were some of the words used against him. But as was always the case he refused to be browbeaten into a course of action which he did not think sensible especially in view of the circumstances in which we found ourselves. And he was supported by the British camp management who welcomed any diversion that would reduce the tensions within the camp. Even so, only about ten men left the camp to work in the community.

✳✳✳

By now the German police, the only authority in our camp apart from the Kommandant, were satisfied that the deportees were unlikely to try to escape. Longer walks were introduced in an endeavour to reduce in-camp fighting over food and petty squabbles. Internees would choose something from the Red Cross parcel to try and trade with the locals for a rabbit or chicken or maybe even a bottle of Schnapps. And everybody searched the hedgerows for additions to their spartan diet. Chickweed tasted like baby sweetcorn and pea shoot. Both the aniseed, peppery Yarrow and young plantain were bitter brassicas. While hawthorn leaves were bread and cheese. All of these provided flavour and taste to mask the appalling and often contaminated food.

The few that volunteered to work locally all agreed that apart from a few perks they took back to the camp the main benefit was getting away from the constant bickering and quarrelling.

For those who had volunteered to work for the locals they were allowed out with the minimum of supervision.

✳✳✳

My father was assigned to work in the gardens of the Families Schoeck and Haug with the children being responsible for collecting and returning him from and to the camp. Sometimes it was Marianne Schoeck who came to the gate and hand in hand they would go off together. At other times it was Peter Haug and although there was no hand holding there was a polite and companionable acknowledgement. It was no surprise that my father soon became friends with both families. He was courteous, well-spoken and with a smattering of German picked up during his travels on the continent managed to communicate in a simple manner. Add to which he was a good worker and they quickly realised how lucky they had been. They made him welcome sharing their acorn coffee with him in the morning and sending him back with a few tomatoes and occasionally some vegetables. I wonder how much that must have hurt, thinking of his destroyed crops and land back home in Guernsey. But I remember Auntie Ol being highly delighted with the tomatoes and on another occasion a couple of eggs. The most amazing of all was when they gave him two white bread rolls. My father gave them in return a little chocolate and some marmalade from his Red Cross parcel. He helped Marianne with her English homework. Strange that in wartime she should be learning English. Sometimes they played the piano together. That was strange too. Although he had bought my mother a baby grand he had shown no interest in it himself. As far as I know he couldn't play a note. Or was it that in the light of everything that had happened and when he so needed love and affection that what he longed for was something which would link him to my mother? Whatever it was, it forged a friendship that was to last long after the war and remains to this day although continued by the children of the original parties.

✻✻✻

The news of D-Day filtered through and with it the feeling that the tide of war had really turned and that although it might take time, at last it was going to happen. Freedom. For the deportees there was joy at the prospect but fear that right at the end, after all those terrible years, they might die in the onslaught that was inevitable the closer the allies got to Germany.

✻✻✻

I remember the relentless raids, the continuous drone of heavy aircraft, the scream of bombs, the barrage of anti-aircraft fire, the sound of big guns and the fear that went with having nowhere to hide. I would get close to Auntie Ol and hide my face in her jumper. Some of the women prayed aloud and all of us feared for the lives of the men on the other side of the barbed wire. But there was also the conviction that it was only by experiencing this that we would ever be free. We had become used to the sounds and sights of Messerschmitts and Focke-Wulfs but now we were listening to the rich purring of the Lancaster with its Rolls Royce engines and capacity for heavy bombing. Sometimes the sky was fiery red and my father would tell me Ulm was burning. It was only after the war that I learned about towns all over the United Kingdom that had been subjected to that kind of attack and that many had burned in exactly the same way. When the bombing grew closer and Biberach was under intense fire my father worried greatly about his new friends the Schoecks and the Haugs.

✳✳✳

As the bombing increased and the allies grew closer conditions in the camp deteriorated again. Walks were discontinued due to the frequency of the bombing and because the locals, now that they faced invasion on their own soil, no longer wanted deportees wandering around their town, nor did they want them gathering wood for their fires. They too were short of fuel. In the camp the meagre food ration became even less and was no longer supported by Red Cross parcels it being too difficult to transport them through war-torn Germany. Hot showers were reduced to one every three weeks. Toilet paper was non-existent, the factory producing it had been bombed. The only consolation was that the people of Biberach were experiencing the same hardships as those in the camp. Little food and no fuel. Everything was being sent to the front in a last attempt to turn the tide in Germany's favour.

Gradually the fighting moved closer. As the all clear sounded for one air-raid another started. Internees watched in shock as American planes were shot down. But worse was to come as American Marauders flew across the camp, their target, Biberach itself. Villagers were killed or buried alive as the Rauthaus came under attack and the town burst into flames which were easily visible from the camp causing many to fear for their own lives.

And now the bombing was followed by the sound of distant gunfire, becoming louder and closer with the passing of every hour and the whole area suffering heavy bombardment. On Sunday 22nd April, the islanders had the satisfaction of seeing the enemy in full flight, tanks and trucks, armoured cars and marching men.

✳✳✳

There were mixed feelings at this time. Overall was the expectation that our long imprisonment would soon end. It had gone on for so many years that people were reluctant to put their hopes and expectations into words in case it didn't happen and then there was the ever present fear that we might not live to enjoy the peace. The guards were becoming more relaxed but the bombing was more intense and the food was barely enough. We had no interest now in following camp activities and many people lay on their bunks and just waited. I was hungry all the time and had no energy to skip or dance about between the raids which became ever more frequent. We heard the news on radios which had been kept hidden from the German guards right from leaving home. Three radios hidden away and listened to? When and by whom? Wisely this information was never shared with we children but years on I realise that there was much more going on in the camp than I had ever imagined. How on earth did they avoid discovery? Camp inspections and searches were regular and thorough, taking place while we all waited in the compound. And then, right at the end, one of the radios was discovered but by then it was too late to matter and the Kommandant handed it back asking for himself what was the Allied news, or in other words how long had he got left before he needed to get out. In a frenzy of activity, guards left. The curfew was no more. I suppose we could have gone out of the camp if we had not been so afraid of the bombing. I don't think anybody would have stopped us, but where would we have gone? The sound of another bomb going off reminded us that it was not all over yet. We were displaced persons in a foreign land amongst people who had every reason now to hate us in the same way many Guernsey people had felt when the Germans landed. Sounds of battle raged as Germans exchanged fire with the advancing French.

Soon there was a message from the Allied Supreme HQ. We were to stay in our camp and wait for further orders. I can see us now, a bedraggled half-starved little group but all standing eagerly by the gate waiting for the first tanks to come through and willing somebody, anybody, to stop and speak to us. The first to arrive were the French following hard on the German retreat and we rushed forward to welcome them, but they drove their tanks by without a second glance. Disconsolate and overcome with disappointment we returned to our barracks to sit around wondering why we had been ignored. For years we had waited for this moment but had failed to appreciate that we were still very much in the middle of a war zone with the military having many more concerns at that moment than our welfare.

***

Next day an internee cycled over to the French units under the command of General Leclerc and told him that the town of Biberach was open and about the internees of Lager Lindele. Unfortunately he was unaware that there was still a hardcore of German military surrounding the camp itself and waiting in a Red Cross hut ready to open fire with heavy guns as soon as the French tanks appeared. The civilians might have thought their war was over but for still serving soldiers it was seen as their duty to fight to the bitter end.

***

Desperate now to be seen by the French we put anything white on the barbed wire and Auntie Ol got out the Union Jack she had hidden right through the war in my mattress. The Germans retreated and the French drove in to loud cheers. It was St. George's Day, the 23rd April when we were liberated, the Nazi flag was removed and to loud cheers the Guernsey Flag, the Flag of England or St. George's Flag, was run up the flagpole. Officers questioned each of us separately and issued us with identity cards. Next day my father and I walked out of the camp together hand in hand. Everywhere there were signs of the recent bombings and of an army that had just retreated.

When the allies entered Bergen Belsen they took photographs of the gas chambers and the piles of skeletal bodies. The pictures were enlarged to giant poster size and pasted up on walls all over the town with one half-way up the hill to our camp. My father stood behind me with his hands pressing down on my shoulders, so that I could not turn away, he made me face it. For some minutes neither of us spoke. It wasn't a complete shock, I had recently witnessed the condition of

Jewish prisoners who had joined us from Bergen Belsen, but the posters spoke of horrors I could never have imagined.

It was so difficult to understand how the German soldiers who had trained their guns on us, herded us around like cattle and been responsible for us nearly starving to death could be the same Germans who had opened their home to my father and were even now welcoming me. But even the worst of our captors seemed nothing like the ones who had committed the kind of atrocities I now saw on the poster. In my child's mind I saw them all. The kindly Rosie Joe who bought milk for our starving babies, the German officers running down the quay with their gifts of chocolate and offers of help for my father, and the guards who had made our lives a misery for the last few years. I wriggled under the continued pressure. 'Dada. Why?'

'There are good and bad in all races,' my father explained, 'but the Germans who did this,' he pointed to the poster, 'are the worst of their kind.' he held me close. 'Margaret, **you** must never let this happen again.' In silence we walked back up the hill our joy at being free diminished.

My father's friends, the Haugs and the Schoecks, were safe and welcomed us warmly. I saw the garden where my father continued to work until we were moved out of the camp, for although we were free we had nowhere to go and indeed it would have been foolhardy to try.

Marianne Schoeck gave me an egg on which she had drawn spring flowers, primroses, violets and pussy willow. It was the loveliest thing I had seen in years and I carried it back holding it in both hands stepping carefully all the way, terrified of dropping it. When I showed *it to Auntie Ol she was equally delighted but for different reasons. She wanted to boil it and eat it right away. I was horrified. My lovely, beautiful egg and even though I was just as hungry as she I didn't want to give it up to a pan of boiling water. For several days we argued about it but eventually I gave in and it was boiled and Auntie Ol and I shared it a spoonful at a time. I quickly forgot about the pretty pictures as I sampled this truly delicious egg.*

✱✱✱

The war ended on the 8th May and the internees stood in the compound to listen to the Prime Minister, Winston Churchill, talk to the nation. At the end of the speech he spoke about "our dear Channel Islands" whose war did not end until the 9th because the German Kommandant refused to surrender.

✱✱✱

From then until the end of June we were in a kind of limbo, waiting for somebody to decide what to do with us. There were Allied soldiers everywhere and lots of people who just seemed to be wandering from one place to another. At least by staying put we felt sure that eventually somebody would notice our existence and come around to dealing with us. The longing to go home was in measure subdued by the weariness and lethargy which followed the long months of exile and deprivation and by the continued lack of food. Sometimes my friend and I would walk into Biberach carrying a packet of cocoa which we hoped to trade for eggs. My father and I visited my mother's grave carrying flowers. I was still unable to understand her behaviour towards me so although I followed my father's example of placing the wild flowers on her grave and joined his prayer I felt remote both from her and the whole period surrounding her death.

***

The internees were loaded into Army trucks together with their few belongings and driven to Mengen Airfield held now by the Americans.

***

We were a pathetic little group, tired and hungry wearing clothes that were falling apart. They were young men, flight-ops weary but still high on adrenalin that comes from winning and seeing the end of a war that had taken the heart out of Europe and had cost the world the lives of many of their comrades. I suppose we were just some of the many they would see in the coming months, but as the trucks came to a halt there was a cheer of welcome and people from everywhere dashing forward to help us down, carrying the children and supporting the old and infirm into the shelter of huge army tents from where I remember the smell of something I hadn't enjoyed in a long time. Food.

And eat it I did, greedily, using both hands and stuffing it into my mouth savouring the rich sweet tastes I hadn't enjoyed in years. Generous hosts delighted in our pleasure showering good things especially on the children. Many of the men had families back home and I saw them shaking their heads at our condition and wondering not for the first time or the last what kind of a monster could do this to the weakest and most vulnerable.

For most of us our pleasure was short-lived. Unused to rich food and in quantity we became extremely unwell, plagued for hours by repeated sickness.

***

For three days the Americans looked after the internees, giving them the best of everything and the finest medical care to start what for some might be a long road to recovery.

***

My father never recovered. He was a broken man, broken in spirit, broken hearted at facing the rest of his life without my mother and with declining health and increasing age unable to restart the business for which he had strived so hard. I saw all this but I never heard him complain or change his mind about the need for a future with hands joined across land and sea. Every year after the war he returned to Biberach to lay flowers on my mother's grave and to visit with the Schoecks and Haugs.

RAF troop Dakotas were sent to take us as we all believed back to dear Sarnia. Seated on facing metal seats with our few belongings dumped on the floor in front of us we waited for the moment of take-off. For most of us it was the first experience of flying and those of us who were not sick enjoyed every moment. The pilot asked me if I would like to sit with him in the cockpit. Would I like? What child would not? A short time later he pointed out 'There they are.' I looked. 'The white cliffs of Dover.' He was excited on my behalf. Politely I responded but my heart was heavy as I realised we were not heading for Guernsey and cliffs that I thought more beautiful, more majestic, than those now facing me.

***

From RAF Northolt they were transported by bus to a Dispersal Centre in Uxbridge for final clearance and the issuing of identity papers, clothing coupons, ration cards and eventually travel warrant cards all of which encouraged them to believe that surely now they were off home. It marked the beginning of months of waiting. The Channel Isles had suffered such deprivation during the war it was impossible to accommodate and provide for more people until conditions improved.

✽✽✽

It was only when we were at last allowed to return home that I began to understand the degree of hardship endured by those who had remained in Guernsey. For those of us who had suffered Dorsten and Biberach I think we had always believed that life at home would have been dramatically different. Different yes, but not in the ways we had imagined. Lives and homes were destroyed. Civilians, like the slaves who battled to build roads and defences, were starved of even basic necessities of food while their German guards knew of no shortage as their food and drink was brought in regularly both by ship and plane. But even that was to change and in the last few months of the war, guards and those they guarded were equally short of food, and now what little the islanders had was shared again between them and their captors. And while everywhere celebrated the peace on 8th May, the Channel Islands remained in captivity until the 9th because the German Kommandant refused to surrender.

In England the peace so long awaited brought its own problems. The hardships which had been accepted because, "There's a war on" suddenly became an inconvenience and caused massive unrest and disappointment. With our hearts set on going back home as soon as we were released we joined the dissatisfied, although not complaining about the food or the luxury of sleeping in a proper bed with soft blankets and crisp clean sheets. Our next-of-kin, my mother's cousin, took my father and me in and with little or no knowledge of how we were feeling set about the business of our rehabilitation as she saw it. Being a teacher she was aghast at how little I had learned during the captivity and devised a programme of catch-up.

Used to obeying orders I went along with whatever she suggested but I remember longing to wander around enjoying the freedom of being able to open a gate and pass through it without a guard shouting and raising his gun. I wanted to sit and look at all the books and magazines. I wanted to eat my meals at a small table just set for four with food in serving dishes and with our being able to help ourselves to a whole potato knowing there might well be another one when that had gone. More than anything I had to get used to the quiet. No bombs, no air raids, no gunfire, no sound of guards shouting at us to roll-call, no dogs looking as if they wanted to tear us to pieces. A return to some sort of formal education seemed yet one more obstacle to climb on the return to normality.

As for my father, freedom meant the right to mourn my mother properly. As long as we were in captivity he felt obliged to keep going for the greater good but now with only me to think about and with even my needs taken care of by a relation there was time for him to retreat into himself. A once proud man, now he had nothing, even the clothes he wore had been donated while the few pounds in his pocket were the kind offerings from public funds.

At last the day came when we were told civilians could go home. With grateful thanks to our cousin and armed with travel passes we *set sail on an overcrowded mail boat, tears in our eyes as we saw Guernsey rising up out of the mist.*

***

It was years after the end of the war that Margaret finally returned to Biberach. Not with an official group but quietly on her own to face some of her complex memories. She revisited the families Schoeck and Haug and with their help placed a bench in memory of her father and his friendship with the two families in a favourite spot overlooking Biberach town. And finally she was able to make peace with her mother and visit her grave to weep for the love they had once shared.

As the years pass the official attitude to the deportation of the islanders becomes one of acceptance. After all, it is argued, it was to be expected during wartime and more a case of "assigned residence" than years of hardship. The few who remain from those days in Dorsten and Biberach know a different story. They were illegally deported civilian hostages and prisoners of war but with no international convention providing safeguards for their treatment. And with no such protection they were placed behind barbed wire, guarded by armed soldiers from watchtowers manned with machine guns and searchlights. Three long years. And German cemeteries bear witness to the forty-five who never returned. Ordinary men, women and children. And while nations pay reparations for crimes against humanity the Channel Islanders alone remain ignored or deliberately forgotten. Was it because this was the crime that should never have been committed and too embarrassing politically for governments to acknowledge?

Today's Margaret is the product of those bitter war years. And if you didn't know her story you would never suspect that she is the guardian of such an amazing tale. You are struck at once by the warmth of her personality, by her ready response to and compassionate understanding of other people. But as you know her better you recognise something else, a steely determination in this loving woman which at once begs the question, is this innate Guernsey? Or was it acquired during those long years in Lager Lindele near Biberach in Southern Germany? One thing is certain. Like her father, Margaret's glass is always half full, never half empty.

It has been my privilege to write the story of Margaret Ruth and Frederick Charles Cockayne, researching the questions Margaret might have asked and drawing some conclusions with what material was to hand. "Beyond the Wire" is therefore a combination of fact and the fiction that comes from supposition.

"We must remember what was done in our names, good or bad, and not be afraid to speak out when necessary but we must always look ahead and not back. The past is gone, we can't change it, but we can move to a good and honourable future with hands joined in friendship."

Frederick Charles Cockayne to his daughter Margaret as they looked at the posters of Bergen Belsen, April 1945

Drusilla Carr is an established writer with traditional publishing houses. Her work under different pseudonyms includes; co-author with her husband of the Daily Mail's number one thriller When the Death Penalty Came Back, Junk Food Hero, Nelson Mandela, Drugs, Sex, Alcohol, Crime and Law, Running a Disco, Throwing a Party, and twenty years spent writing nationally and internationally for major magazines.

Recently published on Amazon are;

Ring of Secrecy. A romantic suspense

Amigo A Collection of 10 Short Stories

Christmas is Always Coming. A seasonal story for children.

She lives and writes on the Isle of Wight in a historic cottage on the coast, loves border collies and is a terrible housewife, preferring to write. She plays bridge badly and loves the theatre, classical music, opera and ballet.

Printed in Great Britain
by Amazon